KEEP IT SIMPLE

KEEP IT SIMPLE

HAZELDEN®

First published October 1989.

Copyright © 1989 Hazelden Foundation.
All rights reserved. No portion of this publication
may be reproduced in any manner without the
written permission of the publisher.

ISBN: 0-89486-625-7
Library of Congress
Catalog Card Number: 89-80792

Printed in the United States of America.

Editor's Note:
   Hazelden Educational Materials offers a variety
of information on chemical dependency and
related areas. Our publications do not necessarily
represent Hazelden or its programs, nor do they
officially speak for any Twelve Step organization.

WE DEDICATE THIS BOOK TO ALL
THOSE WHO'VE GONE BEFORE US AND
CARRIED THE MESSAGE; WE THANK
YOU WITH OUR LIVES

INTRODUCTION

We, the authors of this book, believe a recovery program should be made up of meditation, prayer, and action. This book will try to help readers in each of these areas.

On each page you'll find three sections. The first section will be a quote followed by a few paragraphs on the spiritual message we have found within the quote. We suggest reading the quote and our thoughts on it; then take a few minutes and reflect on your own spiritual journey. How does this quote and our thoughts on the quote speak to your recovery program? Is your program where you want it to be? If so, take pride. If not, think about which of the Twelve Steps you need to work, and what action needs to be taken. We are firm believers that the Steps plus action will solve most problems.

Next on the page, you'll find a Prayer for the Day. We see prayer as an important action. Prayer is an act of reaching outside of yourself. Prayer is an act of asking for help in the task of being human. We suggest reading the Prayer for the Day, and if it fits for you, repeat it throughout the day. If it doesn't, take a few moments and come up with a personal prayer that fits for you. If none comes to mind, use the prayer suggested in Step Eleven, "Thy will be done." Remember, each day we are to turn our self-will over to our Higher Power. In doing so, we get the serenity the program promises.

Finally, you'll find a section named Action for the Day. Our illness was fed by a set of actions. Harmful, destructive actions. A recovery program is also about action. Daily spiritual action. Spiritual action helps us feel better about ourselves and safer in the world. In this section, you'll be asked to take an action that is, we hope, made to strengthen your program. Again, if the action fits, do it. If not, think of one that fits for you.

Also in this book, you'll see that we use words like *addict* and *addiction*. As time changes, so does language. When we use these terms, we are speaking to both the alcoholic and the drug dependent person. We see no difference between the two. We believe both suffer from the same deadly disease. We ask you to see yourself in the pages, and not in any one word.

Recovery is a process of finding balance between mind, body, and soul. Hopefully, this book will help you find or strengthen this balance.

We thank you for letting us share a part of our spiritual journey with you. We wish you well on your spiritual journey. May you and your Higher Power have a wonderful relationship!

THE AUTHORS

***W**e admitted we were powerless over alcohol— that our lives had become unmanageable.*

— Step One
from Alcoholics
Anonymous

*We admitted we were
powerless over alcohol. . .*
— From Step One of
Alcoholics Anonymous

In Step One, we accept our powerlessness over alcohol and other drugs. But we are powerless over many parts of life. We are powerless over other people. We are powerless over what our Higher Power has planned for us.

Before recovery, we only believed in control. We tried to control everything. We fought against a basic truth, the truth that we are powerless over much of life.

When we accept this truth, we begin to see what power we do have. We have the power to make choices. When we're lonely, we have the power to reach out to others. We have power over how we live our own lives.

Prayer for the Day

Higher Power, help me to know that it's You who is running my life. Help me to know that power comes from accepting I am powerless.

Action for the Day

I am powerless over much of life. Today I'll look to see how this is true. I'll look to see what I really have control over and what I don't.

. . .our lives had become
unmanageable.
— Second half of Step One

The First Step tells us a lot about addiction. We were out of control. Our addiction was in control. Addiction managed everything. It managed our relationships. It managed how we behaved with our families. As Step One says, ". . .our lives had become unmanageable."

But we pretended we managed our lives. What a lie! Addiction ran our lives—not us. We weren't honest with ourselves. Our program heals us through self-honesty. We feel better just speaking the truth. We are becoming good people with spiritual values. Our spiritual journey has begun.

Prayer for the Day

Higher Power, I give You my life to manage. When I'm faced with a choice, I'll ask myself, "What would my Higher Power choose for me?"

Action for the Day

Today, I'll be honest with a friend about how unmanageable my life had become.

*Never play leapfrog with a
unicorn.*

> — *Unknown*

As we work Step One, we accept that alcohol
and other drugs are poison to us. We accept
our limits. This means we know that hanging around our drinking or using "buddies"
can remind us of "the good old days." Hanging around "slippery places" means we could
"slip" back into our old ways. This isn't testing
our sobriety; it's being reckless with it.

So, let's accept our limits. Everybody has
limits. When we know our limits, we protect
our recovery against the people and places
that pull us from our spiritual center. This is
what true acceptance means.

Prayer for the Day

I pray for true acceptance. Higher Power, help me
to stay away from slippery places. I will protect the
gift You've given me.

Action for the Day

Today, I'll list the people and places that are risky
for me to be around. I will share this list with my
sponsor, my group, and my sober friends.

*He who is swift to believe is
swift to forget.*
— *Abraham Joshua Herschel*

Life is full of questions. Many people tell us
they have the answers. We have to be careful
of who and what we believe. Other people's
ideas may not fit us.

The program doesn't tell us much about
what to believe. It teaches us *how* to believe.
How well the program works for us depends
on what we believe and how well we live it.

When we face all the facts, we can really
believe. We believe we are powerless over our
addiction. We believe we must and can
change some things in our lives. We believe
we can trust a Higher Power to care for us.
When we choose to believe, we want to choose
the best beliefs we can. And once we believe,
we must not forget.

Prayer for the Day

Higher Power, help me know You, and help me
know the truth.

Today's Action

Today I'll think about my First Step. Do I truly
believe I'm powerless over my disease?

*The journey of a thousand
miles begins with a single
step.*
                    — Chinese proverb

Life holds so many choices now that we are
sober. We'd like to go so many places. We'd like
to see so many things. We have so much to do.

We are slowly learning how to trust our
dreams and reach for them. Our program
teaches us that we live One Day at a Time. We
make progress by doing First Things First.
Easy Does It.

Our dreams may seem very big and far
away. We wonder if we'll ever get there. But
our faith tells us to go for it. And we know
how: one step at a time.

Prayer for the Day

Higher Power, help me know this gentle truth:
my life matters. Help me set goals that I can grow
toward, one step at a time.

Action for the Day

Today I'll think about one of my goals. I will list
ten little steps that will help me get there.

We.
— *First word of the Twelve Steps*

We. This little word says a lot about the Twelve Steps. Our addiction made us lonely. The "we" of the program makes us whole again. It makes us a member of a loving, growing group of people.

Our addiction isolated us from others. We couldn't be honest. We felt a lot of shame. But all this is in the past. The "we" of the program helps us live outside ourselves. Now we tell each other about our pasts. We comfort each other. We try to help each other.

Prayer for the Day

Higher Power, help me to join the *we* of the program. Help me to admit and accept my illness, so the healing can begin.

Action for the Day

Today, I'll work to make the *we* of the program even stronger. I'll find someone to help.

*A good scare is worth more
to a man than good advice.*
— *E. W. Howe*

Do you let yourself be afraid of your illness?
You'd better. Many of us were scared into
sobriety. Often, a spiritual awakening directly
follows a good scare. Fear seems to improve
our vision.

Are you smart enough to run from your addiction? The First Step should create fear
inside us. It's about looking honestly at our
addiction and what would happen to us if we
kept using. Looking at Step One regularly will
give us the respectful fear we need to stay
sober. Often fear is seen as bad, but it can be
good, if we listen to it. It can be a great mover.
When you're afraid, your spirit is trying to tell
you something.

Prayer for the Day

God, direct my fear. Have me go to You, family,
friends, and others who love me. Help me see my
fear and listen to its message.

Action for the Day

I'll list five ways that my fear has taught me important lessons. I'll see that my fear can help me
as long as I listen to it and not live in it.

*Believe more deeply. Hold
your face up to the Light,
even though for the
moment you do not see.*
— Bill W.

At times, we'll go through pain and hardship. At times, we'll have doubts. At times, we'll get angry and think we just don't care anymore. These things can spiritually blind us. But this is normal. Hopefully, we'll be ready for those times. Hopefully, we will have friends who will be there for us.

Thank God for these moments! Yes, hard times can make our spirits deep and strong. These moments tell us who we are as sober people. These moments help us grow and change. Spirituality is about choice. To be spiritual, we must turn ourselves over to the care of our Higher Power.

Prayer for the Day

God, help me find You in my moments of blindness. This is when I really need You.

Today's Action

Today I'll get ready for the hard times ahead. I will list my friends who will be there for me.

*Everything is funny as long
as it is happening to
someone else.*
— *Will Rogers*

We laugh when others do something silly.
We're amused when something funny happens
to them. But if the same happens to us and
people laugh, we might give them the evil eye.

Yet, when others laugh, it can free us. It
frees us to see the world through new eyes.
Likewise, when we laugh at ourselves, we're
free to see ourselves with new eyes. Instead
of trying to be perfect, we accept we're human.
To laugh at ourselves is to accept ourselves.
There's no room for shame when we laugh.
We enjoy ourselves just as we are. Can I accept
the fact I'm human and I have limits?

Prayer for the Day

Higher Power, when I refuse to accept that
I'm only human, be gentle with me. I know that,
when I least expect it, You will remind me that I'm
only human.

Action for the Day

I will share with a friend one or two stories about
funny mistakes I've made.

*I'm always ready to learn,
although I do not always
like being taught.*
— *Winston Churchill*

We addicts are used to learning the hard
way. Many of us think we're different and can
do things our own way. But then we get in too
much trouble or pain. The first A.A. members
were just like us. They knew how it is to hate
being told what to do. So they suggested we
follow the Twelve Steps. They didn't say we
have to do anything. They didn't say working the Steps is the *only* way to live sober.
They just said the Steps worked for them.

We're finding out that the Steps work for us
too. We don't *have* to work them. We don't
have to stay sober. We just like our new sober
life better than our old drinking or drugging
life. And we're learning how to live this new
life by working the Steps.

Prayer for the Day

Higher Power, help me be open to your lessons.
Teach me gently and help me listen.

Action for the Day

I will list five ways that I get in the way of my
own learning.

*If there's a harder way of
doing something, someone
will find it.*
— *Ralph E. Ross*

When we used alcohol or other drugs, we did most things the hard way. We could turn a simple task into a day-long project. We could turn a simple problem into an argument. We were creative giants in doing things the hard way!

We need to change this. We deserve easier lives. It's okay to take the smooth road. In our program, we have slogans for this: Keep It Simple, Let Go and Let God, First Things First, and Easy Does It. These slogans remind us that it's okay to live with as little trouble as possible.

Prayer for the Day

Higher Power, show me how to live a simple life. I don't have to do everything the hard way if I listen better to You.

Action for the Day

I'll list three or four things I do that make my life harder than it needs to be. I'll share them with a friend.

*Remember always that you
have not only the right to
be an individual, you have
an obligation to be one.*
— *Eleanor Roosevelt*

When we were using alcohol and other drugs, we often thought that we were different from others. We secretly thought that no one could understand us. Maybe we tried to be one of the group, but we were lonely.

Now we know for sure—we *are* different from others. Everyone's unique. We all have this in common. Being like others helps us feel safe and normal. But we need to feel good about the ways we're different from others too. We think a little different, act a little different, and look a little different from anyone else. We each have our own way to make life better for others.

Prayer for the Day

Higher Power, help me be an individual. Help me use my special gifts, not hide them.

Action for the Day

Today, I'll make a list of the things I'm good at. I'll think about how I can use these gifts.

*The junkie can never start to
cure himself until he
recognizes his true condition.*
— *Malcolm X*

Now we know what the problem is. Now we
can do something about it. The truth of our
problem is, we can't handle alcohol or other
drugs. They handle us. They control us. The
Steps ask us to face the truth. And the truth
sets us free. What a wonderful gift! We feared
the truth, but now it's our friend. It's a relief.
Facing the truth means we're honest. And
honesty is our best friend in recovery. It's like
a cozy fire on a winter's night. Honesty is how
we get well. It's also what will keep us well.
Do I truly believe I can't use alcohol or other
drugs?

Prayer for the Day

Higher Power, help me see my illness for what
it is. It's my enemy. Help me see that honesty is
my best friend.

Action for the Day

Today, I'll take fifteen minutes to think about
what my *true* condition was when I was drinking
and drugging. And I'll think about what my true
condition is now.

*If you play with a thing
long enough, you will
surely break it.*
— *Anonymous*

Some things shouldn't be played with. Our recovery program is one of these things. When we play with our program, we're taking a risk. We play with the program by missing meetings. Or by not calling our sponsors. Or by skipping the Steps we think are too hard.

It's okay to play. But it's not okay to play with our recovery program. When we play with our program, we risk our lives.

Prayer for the Day

Higher Power, help me know that I must work this program with care and respect.

Action for the Day

Today, I'll make two lists. On one list, I'll write ways I *work* on my program. On the other list, I'll write ways I *play* with my program. And I'll put my energy into working the program.

> *I shall tell you a great*
> *secret, my friend. Do not*
> *wait for the last judgment,*
> *it takes place every day.*
> — *Albert Camus*

"Later." How often have we said this? This trick helps us avoid the tasks of the day. Life is full of tasks—many fun, some boring, others hard. Can I accept the tasks my Higher Power gives me, easy or hard?

When we used alcohol or other drugs, we'd avoid tasks, if they became hard for us. We believed we had more control than we really did. We started to believe we could control outcomes. What we really were doing was setting ourselves up for a great fall. We had to face the fact that when our Higher Power had given us a task, we said no, and turned away. Thus, we turned away from the guiding hand of our Higher Power.

Prayer for the Day

God, help me face You and the tasks You give me. Make me a grateful student of life.

Today's Action

Today I will talk with friends. I will tell them what tasks I'm working on.

> *Fair play is primarily not*
> *blaming others for anything*
> *that is wrong with us.*
> — *Eric Hoffer*

It's tempting to blame others for our problems. Recovery asks us to answer for our actions. Admitting we are powerless over our alcohol and other drugs is a start. Each of the Twelve Steps asks us to answer for our actions in some way. And the program shows us how to do this.

Over time, we see that being responsible for our actions is the best way to live. Our self-confidence grows as we become more responsible. We start to see just how much we can do. We have gone from being drunks to being responsible people. If we can do this, then we can do anything!

Prayer for the Day

I pray to remember that I'm responsible for my actions. Blaming puts distance between me and other people. Higher Power, help me to play fair.

Action for the Day

Today, I'll list four times I've blamed someone else for a problem that was really *my* problem.

*When all else fails, read
the instructions.*
　　　　　　　　— *Agnes Allen*

The instructions for recovery are in our Twelve Step program. Yet, there are times when we feel our program isn't working. At these times, we need to read the instructions.

Have you followed the "instructions," the wise words found in The Big Book, The Twelve and Twelve, and other recovery literature? When we do, we recover.

It's hard at times, and easy at others. Our problems go deeper than just staying sober. No matter what our problems, our program can help us start fixing them, if we follow the instructions. Don't use alcohol or other drugs. Go to meetings. Talk often with sponsors and program friends. Work the Steps. Think. Easy Does It. First Things First. Listen. Let Go and Let God. One Day at a Time.

Prayer for the Day

Higher Power, tell me which instructions to read today. If I'm headed for trouble, help me out.

Today's Action

I'll read the instructions today.

*The reality is that changes
are coming. . . .They must
come. You must share in
bringing them.*
— *John Hersey*

Change. It's scary. It's hard. It's needed.
Sometimes it feels good; other times it feels
bad. But one thing is for sure: it keeps on
happening.

Just when our life seems settled, it
changes. We can't stop life. We can't stay
this age forever. The world changes. Life
moves on. There are always new things to do
and learn.

Change means we're always beginners in
some ways. We need to ask for wisdom and
courage. We get it by listening, by praying, by
meditating. When we ask, our Higher Power
will teach us to be part of good changes.

Prayer for the Day

Higher Power, help me believe that Your plans
call for good changes.

Action for the Day

Today I'll think about the changes in my life. I've
lived through a lot. I'll be okay when more changes
come, with God's help. I can keep on growing.

*Study sickness when you
are well.*
— *Thomas Fuller*

Now is the time to learn about our
sickness—chemical dependency. It is a
chronic illness. That means it never goes
away. We have to live with it the best we can.
Luckily, we *can* live with it—very well! Our
program of recovery is so simple, and it feels
so good, that we think we'll never give it up.
But we can't take our recovery for granted.

Our disease is "cunning, baffling, powerful." The more we know about it, the less we'll
let it fool us. Some days we may find we're
headed toward a slip. We must learn to recog-
nize the first trouble signs in ourselves so we
can get help to stay sober.

Prayer for the Day

Higher Power, my addiction is "cunning, baffling, powerful." Don't let me use alcohol or other
drugs again. Thank you for my sobriety today.

Action for the Day

Today, I'll learn my warning signs: I'll list ten old
thoughts, feelings, and actions that were part of
my illness. I'll share this with my sponsor.

*SERVICE—A beautiful word
fallen upon bad days.*
— *Claude McKay*

Service is really a beautiful word. Service means *respect*. When we serve others we're part of the human race. We all need to help each other.

Service is a sure way to stay sober. Helping someone else stay sober helps us stay sober. And service frees us from self-will. It teaches us about how to care for ourselves and others. It teaches us that we're worthwhile. It teaches us that we make a difference. Service keeps us feeling good.

Am I quiet when the topic of service comes up at meetings? If so, how can I change this?

Prayer for the Day

Higher Power, show me where I can be of help. Give me the courage to make a difference. Give me the courage to really serve others in need.

Action for the Day

I'll list five ways service has made or can make my life better.

*What is defeat?. . .Nothing
but the first step to
something better.*
— Wendell Phillips

A man walks into a meeting. He says, "I surrender. I can't drink like other folks." We smile and welcome him. We know that feeling. All of us in the program must admit defeat. Our illness is more powerful than we are. We begin recovery when we surrender.

Admitting defeat is our first step into a beautiful world. Like all first steps, it's hard. But what a world we find ourselves in! A world where we count! A world where all are really equal!

This first step brings us into God's world of care. We get love. We give love. We stay sober because daily we admit defeat.

Prayer for the Day

I surrender. I can't drink and use other drugs. I'm different. Higher Power, help me surrender daily.

Action for the Day

Every so often, I need to admit defeat and talk about what it was like, what happened, and where I am now.

*Go often to the house of
your friend: for weeds soon
choke up the unused path.*
    — *Scandinavian proverb*

Our program has two parts: the Steps, and
the fellowship. Both keep us sober. We can't
stay sober if we go it alone. We need to work
the Steps. We also need people—the help of
our friends daily.

Recovery is about relationships. We get new
friends. We get involved. We give. We get. In
times of need, we may not want to ask our
new friends for help. Maybe we don't want to
"burden them." Maybe we're afraid to ask for
help. Well, go ahead. Make that call. Ask your
new friend to spend time with you. You
deserve and need it. They deserve it; they
need it.

Prayer for the Day

Higher Power, help me to get help from my
friends as if my life depends on it.

Action for the Day

Today, I'll see or call two program friends and let
them know how I'm doing.

Sex, like all else between human beings, is never perfect.
— *Theodore Isaac Rubin*

Addiction made our sex lives a mess. Maybe we wanted perfect sex or we wanted no sex. We were afraid. Maybe we wanted a high from sex we just couldn't seem to get. Some of us had lots of sex partners; some of us had none.

What now?

We're doing what we need to do by being in recovery. We're getting to know ourselves. We're living by our real values. We're being honest with ourselves and others. We're learning to love and care about others. It's open, honest caring we express with our bodies. Thus, sex can be trusting and safe.

Prayer for the Day

Higher Power, I turn over my sex life and my will to You—just for today. I know You want me to be happy.

Action for the Day

What do I believe about sex? How does it match with what's said in the third paragraph above?

*Few people can be happy
unless they hate some
other person, nation, or
creed.*
— *Bertrand Russell*

In recovery we learn to give up hate. We must stand for justice, not for hate. We must learn to respect people. They, in turn, will respect us in most cases. We begin to see how important it is to give up hate—if we want others to care for us.

Hate is often our secret. Hate is found deep in our hearts and minds. It eats at our souls. It hurts our spiritual growth. Sometimes people are public about their hate. There are even dangerous groups based on hate. But, the most dangerous hate is the private and unspoken. Do I have public hates? Do I have secret hates?

Prayer for the Day

Higher Power, search my heart and show me any hates I have. Help me rid myself of them.

Action for the Day

I'll list any people, nations, or creeds I hate. I'll pray to have this hate removed. I'll pray for these people, nations, or creeds.

*The best place to find a
helping hand is at the end
of your own arm.*
— *Swedish proverb*

During our illness, we hurt others. We hurt ourselves. We messed up a lot. So, a lot of us come into recovery not trusting ourselves very much. The truth is, as addicts, we couldn't be trusted.

But in recovery, we can be trusted again. We can again live and love ourselves. We do this by finding our spiritual center. This is the place inside of us where our Higher Power lives. We turn our will and our lives over to this spiritual center. We do as our spiritual center tells us. And from our spiritual center, we'll find our values. We'll live better lives. We'll come to trust ourselves again.

Prayer for the Day

Higher Power, thank-you for helping me believe in myself again. I'll treat myself with love and kindness. I know You want me to.

Action for the Day

Today, I'll list four ways I couldn't be trusted during my addiction. I'll also list four ways I can now be trusted.

One forgives to the degree
that one loves.
　　　— *La Rochefaucould*

We all get hurt by other people sometimes. When this happens, we have choices. We can get angry and stay that way. We can act like it didn't hurt and try to forget it. We can act like a sad sack and hold a grudge. Or we can forgive.

We first have to think about how someone hurt us. It often helps to talk to the person, to tell the person that he or she hurt us. We then tell the person what we'd like from him or her to help set our relationship straight. Then we let go.

This is what forgiveness is: (1) loving ourselves enough to stand up for ourselves, (2) loving others enough to point out their behavior, and (3) letting go.

Prayer for the Day

Higher Power, help me lovingly forgive those who have hurt me.

Action for the Day

I will list five persons who have hurt me. Have I forgiven them? I will talk to my sponsor about it today.

They are able because they
think they are able.
                    — Virgil

For most of us, addiction was full of doubt. We stopped believing in ourselves. Our thoughts had turned to "stinkin' thinkin'." We didn't believe in much of anything. We didn't take risks. We always looked for the easier, softer way.

In recovery, we start to believe again. We believe in the program. We believe in a Higher Power. We believe in people. And, over time, we believe in ourselves again. We become better at taking risks.

We are able to stay sober because we believe, because we take risks. As we stay sober, we can face almost anything—with the help of others.

Prayer for the Day

Higher Power, I have learned to believe in You. Help me believe in myself. I have something to give to this world. Help me give it freely.

Action for the Day

Today, I'll list ten good points about myself. I'll go over these good points with a friend.

There is no they, only us.
    — Bumper sticker

We're now part of a fellowship we call "the program." Let's also remember that we're part of a larger fellowship called "the human race." We all hurt the same. We all love the same. We all bleed the same. We all need understanding and care.

Yet, in other ways, we are *not* all the same. Let's remember to understand differences among people. If not, we'll be afraid of anyone who's not like us. And this isn't God's way.

Prayer for the Day

Higher Power, help me to love all people. Help me be open to others who are different from me. Help me love my neighbor.

Action for the Day

Do I think I'm better than others? If that's true, I'll pray that my Higher Power will remove this shortcoming of mine.

*An alcoholic spends his life
committing suicide on the
installment plan.*
     — Laurence Peter

None of us woke up one morning and found we had suddenly turned into an addict. We got to be one by practice. And we practiced often. We ignored our families—we left work early—and went drinking and drugging. Daily, we chose chemicals over anything else.

Likewise, getting sober is no accident. We use the Steps. We work the program. At meetings, we're reminded to help others. We all get sober on the installment plan. A day at a time. We got sick one day at a time; we recover one day at a time.

Prayer for the Day

Today, with my Higher Power's help, I'll be happier, more honest, more sober. Sobriety is like a good savings account. Higher Power, help me to put in more than I take out.

Action for the Day

I'll go over my Step One to remind myself it's no accident I'm an addict.

Go and wake up your luck.
    — Persian proverb

We've been given recovery. For this, we're lucky. And we're grateful. Now it's up to us. We must accept our choices. When we're afraid, do we choose to be alone? Or do we choose to go to an extra meeting? When we're not honest, do we keep it secret? Or do we admit it and try to be more honest? No matter what we choose, we're responsible for that choice. Through choices, we either make our program strong or weak.

We can choose to be lucky. Or we can choose not to be. The choice is ours. Our addiction robbed us of choice. It taught us to blame others. Now we see ourselves as responsible.

Prayer for the Day

Higher Power, help me to choose wisely. Help me remember I'm responsible for my choices.

Today's Action

Today I'll work at being responsible for my choices. I'll see myself as one of the lucky ones.

*Do not cut down the tree
that gives you shade.*
— Arabian proverb

We need to remember what got us well. The
Twelve Steps heal us. The meetings we attend
heal us. Reading and listening to program
tapes heal us. Talking with our sponsor heals
us. The time we spend with program friends
heals us.

Sometimes we're pressed for time. As a
result, we have to make choices about how to
use our time. We may think we know enough
about the program. We may feel like cutting
down on meetings. These are danger signs.
We only know how to stay sober One Day at
a Time: by working the Steps. Let's not forget them as we grow in this program. It may
seem like we've been recovering a long time,
but we're all beginners.

Prayer for the Day
Higher Power, I've found You in the program.
Help me find ways to stay a "beginner" in the
program.

Action for the Day
Today, I'll take time to read the Twelve Steps. I'll
meditate on how much these Steps have given me.

February

*C*ame to believe
that a Power greater
than ourselves could
restore us to sanity.

— *Step Two*
from Alcoholics
Anonymous

> *Came to believe that a*
> *Power greater than*
> *ourselves could restore us*
> *to sanity.*
> — *Step Two*

The Second Step directs us to believe there is hope for us. It may take time to believe this. Many of us had given up hope. But look around. Hope fills our meeting rooms. We are surrounded by miracles. This Power greater than ourselves has healed many. Listen as others tell their stories. They speak of how powerful this Power is.

At times, we will not want to believe. This is normal. But in recovery, "coming to believe" means opening ourselves up to healing power found in the program.

Prayer for the Day

Higher Power, allow me to believe. Help me stay open to recovery.

Action for the Day

I will list three examples of my past insanity. I will share these examples with my group, sponsor, a program friend, or with my Higher Power. I will remember that I'm a miracle.

*We must believe the things
we teach our children.*
— *Woodrow Wilson*

It may be easy to say the words and phrases we've heard without really meaning them. Someone says something at a meeting that sounds good. Our counselor has a favorite saying. We may say these words, but are we taking the time to ask the question, Do I believe what I'm saying?

Step Two speaks of, "Came to believe...." By really believing in the Twelve Steps, we let them become part of us. The more we believe in the Steps the more we turn our lives over to them. Hopefully, over time, the Twelve Steps will guide us more and more. We'll speak to our family with the respect we've found in the Twelve Steps. Our spirit must truly believe. Then we can work the Steps.

Prayer for the Day

Higher Power, believing is something that lasts a lifetime. Give me the power to believe even when doubt creeps in.

Action for the Day

My beliefs are changing. Today, in my inventory, I'll ask: Do I believe what I said today?

Never go to a doctor whose
office plants have died.
— *Erma Bombeck*

We often hear, "Stick with the winners." Not everyone in Twelve Step meetings is there for recovery. But many members follow a Twelve Step way of living. We need to find those people. This is really true when it comes to finding a sponsor.

Look for a sponsor who gets good things from his or her program. Why pick a sponsor who isn't happy in the program? Recovery is hard work. You deserve the best. Find the best sponsor you can. Remember, ours is a selfish program. We're fighting for our lives.

Prayer for the Day

Higher Power, help me find the best in my program. Help me find a good sponsor, so we can get as much from each other and this program as we can.

Today's Action

Today I'll think about what it means to have a good sponsor.

*We do not remember days,
we remember moments.*
— *Cesare Pavese*

It's the moment that's important. Each moment holds choice. Our spirits grow through working our program moment to moment. Moments lead to days, days to years, and years to a life of honest recovery.

It will be the moments of choice that we remember. The moment we call a friend instead of being alone. The moment we decide to go for a walk instead of arguing with our partner. The moment we decide to go to an extra meeting instead of drinking or using other drugs. These moments lead us to our Higher Power. These moments teach us that we're human, that we need others. At these moments, we know others care about us— our joys, and our struggles.

Prayer for the Day
Higher Power, help me remember that my recovery is made up of many moments of choice.

Today's Action
I'll look back over the last twenty-four hours. What moments come to mind? Why were they important to me?

Do not bite at the bait of
pleasure til you know there
is no hook beneath it.
— Thomas Jefferson

Pleasure is important in recovery. But at times we think pleasure is the answer to life's pains. Alcohol and other drugs were what we liked best. We need to watch out so we don't switch to another addiction—such as gambling, food, sex, or work.

The real answer to life's pains is in having a strong spiritual center. It is also our best way to avoid another addiction. Recovery lets us turn our pain over to the *care* of our Higher Power. Our Higher Power can handle any problem we may have. Our program can help us with our problems too. Recovery is a three-way deal—Higher Power, program, and us.

Prayer for the Day
Higher Power, help me avoid another addiction. When I have problems, have me come to You and to my program before anything else.

Action for the Day
Today, I'll set aside time and ask the question, "Am I headed for another addiction?" I'll also ask my sponsor what he or she thinks.

We will not know unless we begin.

— *Howard Zinn*

Let us begin! Whether it be working on our First Step, finding a sponsor, or talking to someone we've hurt—let us begin. Doubt will set in if we wait too long. Fear will follow. So, let us begin.

We learn by doing. Recovery is for doers. Sobriety doesn't just happen. We create it. We create it by working the Steps and learning from them. We'll never totally understand the Steps unless we work them. In the same way, we'll never learn how to have friends unless we try. So, call your friends, instead of waiting to be called. Begin and begin again. Each day *is* a new beginning.

Prayer for the Day

Higher Power, today I'll begin. I begin by asking for Your help and love. Be with me as I go through my day. Help me work for progress, not perfection.

Action for the Day

Today, I'll not sit on the sidelines. I'll be a doer. I'll decide what to do to move closer to friends, family, Higher Power, and myself.

*I thank God for my
handicaps, for through
them, I have found myself,
my work and my God.*
   — Helen Keller

None of us ever wanted to be addicts. It's not what we would choose to be—just as no one would choose to be blind and deaf. Helen Keller, who was blind and deaf, told of how her problems became her biggest gift. Through them, she found true meaning in her life.

We can accept our handicap—our addiction—and learn from it. The truth is, we're all handicapped in some way. Recovery is about facing our addiction and learning to live with it. When we see we can't do things alone, we see the need for a Higher Power.

Prayer for the Day

Higher Power, help me see myself as I really am. Give to me the serenity that comes from accepting my handicaps.

Action for the Day

Today, I'll list all the ways I am handicapped. I'll ask myself, "What gift does each of these hold for me?"

*You must find the ideas
that have some promise in
them...it is not enough to
just have ideas.*
— *George E. Woodberry*

Each day we're flooded with ideas. Everyone seems to have found the truth, and now they want to share it. We may feel loaded down with all these ideas. Who and what do we believe?

We've fallen on a set of ideas that hold great promise: The Twelve Steps. The ideas of the program have much promise because they're simple. They ask nothing that isn't good for us. They have been proven to work. Now we're people with more than ideas. We're people with good ideas that *work*. When we find ourselves wondering how to live, all we need to do is look to the Steps.

Prayer for the Day

Higher Power, help me to put my energy into working the Steps.

Action for the Day

Today, I'll list what is right about the Steps for me. What promises do the Steps hold for me?

H.A.L.T.

— AA Slogan

H.A.L.T. stands for Hungry, Angry, Lonely, and Tired. These feelings can be of danger to us. They can lead us away from our program.

We need to eat regular meals. When we get too hungry, we get cranky. Then we say and do things we regret.

We need to turn anger over to our Higher Power, or else our anger can turn into rage.

We need friends to help us in recovery. If we get too lonely, we may turn to our addictive ways for friendship. We don't stay sober by ourselves.

We need a clear mind to deal with life. If we get too tired, we tend to feel sorry for ourselves. Being tired gets us into crazy thinking.

Prayer for the Day

Higher Power, remind me to H.A.L.T. Help me to not get too Hungry, Angry, Lonely, or Tired.

Action for the Day

Today, I'll review the four parts of H.A.L.T. In which areas do I practice good self-care? In which areas do I not? How can I improve?

*Life didn't promise to be
wonderful.*
— *Teddy Pendergrass*

Life doesn't promise us anything, except a chance. We have a chance to live any way we like. No matter how we choose to live, we'll have pain and we'll have joy. And we can learn from both.

Because of our recovery program, we can have life's biggest wonder—love. We share it in a smile, a touch, a phone call, or a note. We share it with our friends, our partners, our family. Life didn't promise to be wonderful, but it sure is full of little wonders! And we only have to open up and see them, feel them, and let them happen.

Prayer for the Day
Higher Power, help me see the wonders of life today, in nature, in people's faces, in my own heart.

Action for the Day
I can help make wonderful things happen for others, with a smile, a greeting, a helping hand. What "little" things will I do for someone today?

*Sanity is madness put to
good use.*
— *George Santayana*

In Step Two we come to believe a Power greater than ourselves can restore us to sanity. In a way, as we work Step Two, we're praying that our madness can be put to good use. This is just what happens. Addiction was wrecking our life. But it's also our addiction that forced us into a new way of life.

As long as we remember what our madness was like, we can put it to good use. When we feel like giving up, let's remember our madness. It will help us go on. When we see someone suffering from the illness of addiction, let's remember our own days of madness. It will help us be there for that person. It's also good to remember that our madness is only a pill or a drink away.

Prayer for the Day

Higher Power, I believe You can put my madness to good use. I give up my madness; do with it what You want.

Action for the Day

I'll list a couple ways my Higher Power and I have changed my madness into sanity.

*We are always the same
age inside.*
— *Gertrude Stein*

Deep inside, we each have a child's spirit. We still have many of the feelings we had when we were young. Some of us have a hurting child inside. There's sadness, fear, or anger that hasn't gone away. We're still lonely, no matter how many people care about us.

Our inner child needs special help to heal. We can be good parents to our inner child. We do this by being gentle and caring with ourselves. In time, this child can be a happy center in our hearts.

Prayer for the Day
Higher Power, please heal the child inside me a little more each day. Help my inner child be alive, free, and full of joy.

Action for the Day
Right now, I'll close my eyes for a minute. I'll think kind thoughts about myself. Then I'll say out loud, "Inner child, I love you. I'll take good care of you." I'll do this two more times today.

Tomorrow doesn't matter,
for I have lived today.
> — *Horace*

Life is found in the present. One of the first things we hear when we enter the program is, One Day at a Time. We break life into short time periods. This gives us the power to change. We're not sure we can stay sober for a lifetime. But we know that with God, and our program, we can stay sober for today.

This holds true for many other things in our lives. We're not sure we can go a lifetime without feeling self-pity, but we can give it up for the day. By living One Day at a Time, we become more sure of our strength. We have the power to change things only in the present. The present holds much for us, if we get a hold on it.

Prayer for the Day

Higher Power, You are found in the moment. You are here. I will stay with You minute by minute.

Action for the Day

I will ground myself in the present. Today, I'll not worry about the past or the future.

*Some things have to be
believed to be seen.*
— *Ralph Hodgson*

In recovery, we learn to trust. We trust that our Higher Power is on our side. Maybe we can't *see* our Higher Power, but once we start trusting, things change. Step Two says, "Came to believe. . ." Once we come to believe, we start to see our Higher Power working in many ways. We make new program friends. We find new peace. Our family and friends trust us again.

Life won't always be fair. We won't get all we want. But we'll find the love and care we need. If we're open to believing in love, the easy times will be easier and the harder times a bit softer. Do I believe in love?

Prayer for the Day

Higher Power, help me believe, especially when times are hard. Help me not blame You for the hard times.

Action for the Day

I will write what I believe the program and my Higher Power want for me.

Easy Does It.
          — Twelve Step slogan

We are people who push ourselves too hard. We try to be perfect. Well, we need to lighten up. Easy Does It. We need to slow down our pace.

Why? Because our program teaches us to give up trying to be perfect. We begin to love ourselves for who we are. *We are enough.* Over and over we hear this as we live the Steps. It's the message of God's love.

Our Higher Power wants us to live at a pace that's not fast and hard, so we always know we're loved. Remember, we've turned our life over to the *care* of God. And our life is a wonderful gift. As recovering people, we may know that better than others.

Prayer for the Day

Higher Power, teach me to live at Your pace, not mine. Help me keep in mind that life isn't a race. It's a spiritual journey. Walk with me.

Action for the Day

Today, I'll take two hours just to relax and do loving things for myself. I'll take time to count my blessings.

*Friendships, like
marriages, are dependent on
avoiding the unforgivable.*
— John D. MacDonald

We need to remember that relationships are made up of people—people who are strong, but also fragile. We don't break easily, but we do break. We need to be aware of how fragile relationships are. Don't say something that will hurt others even if it's honest. It's mean to be honest with someone, without showing that you care for the person's feelings.

We can learn to be honest without being cruel. The backbone of any relationship is this: we need to honor the rules and agreements we make. If we promise to be faithful to someone, we follow this rule. And we need to trust the other person to do the same. When we see that our agreements don't work, we need to go to that person and talk about them.

Prayer for the Day

Higher Power, help me become a person who honors rules and agreements in my relationships.

Action for the Day

I'll make no promises today that I will not keep.

> *. . . no one who learns to*
> *know himself remains just*
> *what he was before.*
> — *Thomas Mann*

Deep inside, we all know that we're changing. It started when we took Step One. We learned and accepted something new about ourselves. That changed us, just a little.

We no longer wanted to live as addicts. That meant we had to change and to learn to live sober. It's been nonstop ever since: learn about ourselves, change a little, learn about ourselves, change a little more, and so on.

All we know is that each step of learning and changing makes life better. How long can it keep getting better? As long as we keep learning to know ourselves.

Prayer for the Day

Higher Power, teach me about myself today. Teach me gently.

Action for the Day

Today, I'll think about what I've learned about myself by working the program. I'll list five things.

*Whoever gossips to you will
gossip about you.*
— *Spanish proverb*

Gossip can kill the trust in a Twelve Step program. We all need to feel safe when we share our personal lives with others. We need to know our private business won't be spread around.

We can do two things to help keep the trust in our groups, and in the rest of our lives too. First, don't gossip. Second, don't listen to gossip about others.

Prayer for the Day

Higher Power, help me mind my own business today. Help me honor the trust of my friends by not gossiping.

Action for the Day

Today, I'll think of two ways to stop someone from telling me gossip. Then, I'll put those ways to use.

*Changing brings questions,
and questions bring
change.*
              — Anonymous

What am I becoming? How do I know if what I'm doing is right? Is it best for me? We are full of questions. Often, times of questions are times of change. We are becoming something new, and there is always a little fear of change.

Luckily, we don't *need* to know what we are becoming to find peace. What we need to know is what we believe in. And we'll become what we believe in. If we believe in sobriety, we'll be sober. If we believe in honesty, we'll struggle to be more honest.

We must give ourselves the freedom of becoming. Becoming means we're on a trip, a journey. Over time, becoming takes on a comfort of its own.

Prayer for the Day

Higher Power, what am I becoming? I give up having to know the answer. All I need to believe is that You love me and will do what is best for me.

Action for the Day

I'll ask lots of questions. Often, the question is more important than the answer.

Let Go and Let God.
— Twelve Step slogan

Some days we might ask ourselves, *Is it worth it?* We feel alone. No one seems to care. Life seems hard. Recovery seems hard.

This is when we need to slow down and take a look at what's going on. We're feeling this way because we're off our recovery path. We may be back into wanting people to see things our way, or do things our way. We want control.

Remember, all problems are not *our* problems. All work is not *our* work. We can't have everything the way we want it. But we can do our part and let go of the rest. Then we can feel better.

Prayer for the Day

Higher Power, help me remember my only work today is to do Your will for me. It is not my job to be You.

Action for the Day

I'll talk with my sponsor or a program friend today. I'll talk about how to deal with things that seem to pull me down.

To thine own self be true.
— AA medallions

Sometimes we hear that we have a "selfish program." Being "selfish" means that we ask for help when we need it. We only go to places that are safe for us, no matter what others are doing. Being selfish comes to mean *safety* for us.

Being selfish doesn't mean we act like brats. We must act in ways that show respect and love—for ourselves and for others. Being selfish means we do what is *good* for us.

What is good for us? First, we have to save our lives by stopping our drinking and drugging. Next, we start working the Steps. We come to know a loving Higher Power. This is how we come to know our true self.

Prayer for the Day

Higher Power, help me be true to myself and my values. Help me be "selfish" about spending time to talk with You each day.

Action for the Day

I'll list ten ways I need to be "selfish" in recovery. If I get stuck, I'll be "selfish" and ask for help.

It's easier to speak of love,
than to practice it.
— Anonymous

Do we help our neighbor who is in need? We must help when we see the need, not just when it fits our schedule. In the program, this becomes our goal. We work at helping out. For example, when someone is needed to run the meeting, we offer. We see that the needs of the group are also our needs. We are the group.

Over time, the idea of service spreads to the rest of our lives. Maybe we help a family down the street. We start to see that we have something to offer the world: ourselves. We start to see that the needs of the world are also our needs. We are an important part of the world.

Prayer for the Day

Higher Power, make me quick to act when I see a need. Please don't let my fear stop me.

Action for the Day

Today, I'll list what I have to offer the world. I will think of two ways I can use these gifts my Higher Power has given me.

Hitch your wagon to a star.
— Ralph Waldo Emerson

Millions of people are sober and have peace of mind through the Twelve Steps. Like the stars, the Steps are always there. At times, clouds block our view of the stars, but we know they're still there. Let's view the Twelve Steps the same way.

It is said that the stars are the gate to heaven, that we pass through their beauty to get ready to enter heaven. The Twelve Steps are the gate to spirituality here on earth. We travel through their beauty on our way to a spiritual awakening. Hitch your wagon to the Steps, and get ready for the ride of a lifetime!

Prayer for the Day

I pray to remember that the Steps keep me sober. I pray that I will follow where the Steps take me.

Action for the Day

I'll look at the stars tonight. I'll think of them as symbols of my life touched by the Twelve Steps.

Failure is impossible.
  — Susan B. Anthony

Failure is an attitude. Having an attitude of failure can't help us. It can only hurt us. If we're not careful, it can grow into a way of life. So, when we feel like failures, we'd better look at our attitudes.

An attitude of failure often comes from making mistakes. But we can learn to see our mistakes as lessons. This turns mistakes into gains, not failures. Sometimes, we try to do things that just can't be done. When we act like we can control others, we're going to fail. When we act like we know everything, we're going to fail. If we try to act like God, we're going to fail.

We can't control others. We can't know everything. We're not God. We're human. If we act human, we've already won.

Prayer for the Day

Higher Power, help me to learn from my attitudes. Whatever the outcome, help me learn.

Action for the Day

Facing our past "failures" is the first step to learning from them. I'll talk to my sponsor about a past "failure" and the good that came from it.

*Believe that life is worth
living and your belief will
help create the fact.*
— *William James*

Step Two speaks of believing. For many years, we had given up believing in ourselves, in a Higher Power, and in others. We believed in getting high.

Now our program tells us to believe in love. We *are* lovable, and we can love others without hurting them.

Of course, believing is an important part of recovery. To believe means to put aside our doubts. To believe means to have hope. Believing makes the road a little smoother. So, believing lets the healing happen a little faster.

All of this is how we get ready to let in the care of our Higher Power.

Prayer for the Day
I pray for the courage to believe. I'll not let doubt into my heart. I can recover. I can give myself totally to this simple program.

Action for the Day
I'll list four times doubt got in my way. And I'll think of what I can do to not let that happen again.

Forewarned, forearmed;
being prepared is half the
victory.
— *Miguel de Cervantes*

There will be hard times in our program. There will be hard times in our life. That's the way life is. It helps if we accept this. Then we can prepare for tough times.

We can prepare by getting a good set of habits and sticking to them. We can make it a habit to give time to our program each day.

Sticking to good habits is like having a savings account: when hard times come, we can take the "investment" we've made and overcome our problems.

Prayer for the Day

Higher Power, help me accept that there will be hard times. Help me prepare for them. With Your help, I'll stay close to You, my friends, and the program.

Action for the Day

I'll put something into my program "savings account" today. I'll make that extra call. I'll read a little longer or go to an extra meeting.

*Without work all life goes
rotten.*
— *Albert Camus*

Work is more than earning money. Work means using our time and skills to make life better for those around us. Our work can be our hobbies. Growing food or growing flowers can be our work. Raising children or caring for older people who need help can be our work. Building homes or helping people live in them can be our work.

Thanks to our program of recovery, we can do our best work again. What a change from the drugged-up and hung over days when we didn't do anything well. We are sober, and we have something to offer.

Prayer for the Day
Higher Power, help me see that work makes me part of the human family. Help me do Your will in my work today.

Action for the Day
Good work teaches us good habits. How do the things I've learned in my work help me in my recovery program? I'll list five ways.

Leave yourself alone.
— Jenny Janacek

We often pick on ourselves. We put ourselves down. But doing this isn't part of our recovery. In fact, it goes against our program. Our program is based on loving care. We have turned our lives over to a caring, loving Higher Power who will give us the answers.

We are told Easy Does It. We back off. As recovering addicts, we learn not to judge. Instead, we learn to be kind to ourselves. Our job is not to figure out the world, but to add more love to it. Let's start with ourselves.

Prayer for the Day

Higher Power, stop me from judging. Help me know what You want me to do. Help me work Steps Two and Three.

Action for the Day

Today, I'll leave myself alone. I will remember that picking on myself is another form of control.

*In my friend, I find a
second self.*
— *Isabel Norton*

We are all part of each other. *We* are part
of others. When we can't see ourselves, maybe
we need to look at others in our group. We can
learn from them. We can learn how to stand
firm, even when our knees are shaking and we
want to run away. We can learn to speak gently to ourselves, even when our heart is full of
tears. We can learn how to take pride in the
simple things we do. Our friends in the program can teach us all these things.

We will learn to love again as others come
to love us. We will become the heaven that
keeps others from the hell of addiction.
Through us, others will believe that a Power
greater than themselves can restore them to
sanity.

Prayer for the Day

Higher Power, please watch over the members
of my Twelve Step group. Keep them safe and sober,
for they have helped to keep me safe and sober.

Action for the Day

I will take time to find some way to say thank-
you to my group.

*M*ade a decision to
turn our will and our
lives over to the care of God
as we understood Him.

— *Step Three*
from Alcoholics
Anonymous

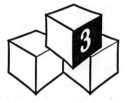

*Made a decision to turn our
will and our lives over to
the care of God as we
understood Him.*
— *Step Three*

Care. This is what we turn our will and lives over to the care of our Higher Power. What peace follows! We see our God as caring, as loving. We turn everything over to this Higher Power, who can take better care of us than we can by ourselves.

Care can guide us. If we want to do something, we can ask ourselves, "Would my Higher Power see this as an act of care?" If the answer is yes, then we go ahead. If the answer is no, we don't do it. If we can't be sure, we wait and talk it over with our friends and sponsor. We wait until we know whether it would be an act of care or not. What wonderful guidance!

Prayer for the Day
Higher Power, I give to You my will. I give to You my life. I gladly jump into Your loving arms.

Action for the Day
Today, I'll care about others. I'll find as many ways as I can to care for others.

*Love conquers all; let us
surrender to love.*

— *Virgil*

In Step Three, we turn our lives over to
God's care, God's love. If we turn our lives over
to a loving God, we can conquer all.

If you need proof, look around at your next
meeting. The room will be full of people who
know that love conquers addiction. Like them,
we've surrendered to love. Once we've done
this, we can't use again. For us, using alcohol or other drugs is an act of hate, not love.

To face the hard things in life, we'll need a
lot of love. We'll find love in our Higher Power,
groups, and friends. We're now part of a community based on love. We're all working at
turning our lives over to love.

Prayer for the Day

There was a time that love scared me. It still
does, at times. Higher Power, help me see that You
are love, and I must follow where love takes me.

Action for the Day

I'll meditate on the question, "How has Step
Three changed my life?"

But the alcoholic. . .will be absolutely unable to stop drinking on the basis of self-knowledge.
— *Alcoholics Anonymous*

Our program says three things are more important than knowing ourselves: (1) admitting we have no control over our addiction, (2) believing in a Higher Power, and (3) turning our lives over to the care of that Higher Power.

Knowing ourselves makes our lives better in recovery. But it does not give us sobriety. Sobriety starts with surrender to our Higher Power. We now know we need the faith and strength we get from a Higher Power. We also need the support of others in our program.

Prayer for the Day

Higher Power, thank you for my sobriety today. Teach me what I need to know about myself to do Your will today.

Action for the Day

Today, I'll talk with my sponsor about the change in my spirit that keeps me sober.

Better bend than break.
— Scottish proverb

Our program is based on bending. We call it "surrender." We surrender our self-will to the care of God. We do what we believe our Higher Power wants us to do. We learn this as an act of love.

Many of us believed surrender was a sign of weakness. We tried to control everything. But we change as we're in the program longer and longer. We learn to bend. We start to see that what is important is learning. We learn to do what's best for us and for others. To learn, we need an open mind. To bend, we must stay open. Love and care become the center of our lives.

Prayer for the Day

Higher Power, teach me that strength comes from knowing how and when to bend.

Action for the Day

Today, I'll check on myself. How open am I? Do I bend when I need to?

I am not afraid of
tomorrow, for I have seen
yesterday and I love today.
— William Allen White

Big changes are happening to us, but we can trust that changes will bring good things. After all, what have we got to lose? We have lived through the days and years of our addiction. Now, with the help of our Higher Power, the pain of those days has ended. We have no reason to worry.

Yet, recovery won't make our lives perfect. Hard things still happen. But we never have to lose hope again. We never have to feel alone with our problems again.

What will come next? We don't know the details, but we can be sure the future will be good if we stay on our path of recovery.

Prayer for the Day

Higher Power, I know life holds many new things for me. Help me and protect me as I live in Your care today.

Action for the Day

Today, I'll trust that each day of my life will bring me good. I will share this idea with one friend.

*When I see a bird that
walks like a duck and
swims like a duck, and
quacks like a duck, I call
that bird a duck.*
— *Richard Cardinal Cushing*

Remember how we tried to make others think we were not in trouble? We walked and talked like addicts. We acted like addicts. Most everyone knew the truth but us. We were like ducks pretending to be eagles.

We need to see ourselves as we really are. But sometimes we can't see ourselves that way. This is normal. That's why we need others to help us see what we can't. We were *addicts*. We are now *recovering addicts*. We need friends, sponsors, and family members to tell us when we may be acting like *addicts* again. It may save our lives.

Prayer for the Day
Higher Power, give my friends and family members the strength to tell me when I'm acting like an addict.

Action for the Day
I'll go to people whom I trust and ask them to tell me when I'm acting like an addict.

To make the world a
*   friendly place*
One must show it a
*   friendly face.*
*   — James Whitcomb Riley*

We are beginning to learn that we get what we expect. Why? If we believe that people are out to get us, we'll not treat them well. We will think it's okay to "get them" before they "get us." Then, they'll be angry and want to get even. And on it goes.

It's great when we can meet the world with a balance. We are now honest people. We can expect others to be fair with us. We get the faith, strength, and courage to do this because of our trust in our Higher Power.

Prayer for the Day

Higher Power, I put my life in Your care. Use me to spread Your love to others.

Action for the Day

Today, I'll spread friendliness. I will greet people with a smile.

*We lose the fear of making
decisions, great and small,
as we realize that should
our choice prove wrong we
can, if we will, learn from
the experience.*

— *Bill W.*

As our disease grew, we often felt like any decision we made was wrong. We felt like *wrong people.* We lost self-respect, because deep inside we knew that, for us, using alcohol and other drugs was wrong. We went against our spirit.

Now we go with our spirit. We follow what we think our Higher Power wants for us. Now we *learn* from our mistakes. Another wonderful gift has been given back to us: the gift of learning. From this gift, we stop playing God. How free it feels!

Prayer for the Day

Higher Power, You have taken away my illness and replaced it with many wonderful gifts. I thank You for everything, even my mistakes.

Action for the Day

Today, I'll share with a friend my mistakes of the past week.

*You've got to do your own
growing, no matter how
tall your grandfather was.*
— *Irish proverb*

Each of us has been given recovery. Now it's up to each of us what we do with it. At times, we'll work hard and grow quickly. At other times, our growth will be slower. This is okay. We're not in a race. Our pace is not important. What is important is that we're always working on our recovery.

We're all part of a fellowship, a caring group. We're one of many. But we're each important. Each one of us will have a special way to work our programs through our readings, friends, meetings, and what we know of how life works. Each of us puts together a miracle of recovery. We then take our miracle and share it with others, so they can build their miracle.

Prayer for the Day

Higher Power, help me work at growing. Help me be a person who is an important part of a group.

Action for the Day

Today, I'll work at seeing myself as very important. I'll remind myself that others' recovery also depends on my recovery. I am needed.

Little things affect little minds.
— *Benjamin Disraeli*

Before recovery, we liked things *our way.* We thought every new thing we tried should go right the first time. Little problems could really upset us. We let little things spoil our day. We let little things affect big things—our entire lives. And our bad moods affected people around us.

Funny how we have fewer of those problems now. The program is teaching us to let go. What a relief when we know we don't have to control every little thing! How nice when things get done without our "expert advice"! We are starting to see what's really important, and what's not. One promise of the program is coming true: we know how to handle situations better.

Prayer for the Day

Higher Power, help me see what is really important for me today. Help me to stop worrying about what's not.

Action for the Day

When I'm upset, I'll ask myself, Is this problem really so bad? If I can't change it, I'll let go.

If it ain't broke, don't fix it.
— AA saying

Before recovery, we never thought we had
enough alcohol or other drugs. More would
make us feel better, we thought. Sometimes,
we are like this in our recovery too. We know
we need to change, so we want to do it all
right now. If we can just change ourselves
totally, we'll feel better, we think.

But we can't change all at once. If we ask
our Higher Power to take charge of our lives,
we'll have the chance to change a little at a
time. We'll learn the right things when we
need to know them.

Prayer for the Day

Higher Power, help me fix what needs fixing
today.

Action for the Day

I'll make a list of what is broken. Which things
on my list can I fix today?

*The Twelve Step program is
spiritual, based on action
coming from love...*
— *Martha Cleveland*

To be *spiritual* means to be an active person. It means spending time with others. It means sharing love. It means looking for ways to be more loving to others. It means looking for ways to make the world a better place.

Step Three helps us to look at the world better. We turn our lives over to the *care* of our Higher Power. So let's allow *care* to direct our lives. Let's always be asking ourselves, "Is what I'm doing something that shows I care?"

Prayer for the Day
Higher Power, let me be active in a loving, caring way. Let the love in my heart be my guide.

Action for the Day
Today, I'll do something good for someone and keep it a secret.

*God loves the world
through us.*
— *Mother Teresa*

In Step Three, we turn our will and our lives over to the *care* of God. How do we feel God's care, God's love? We feel God's care and love through how people treat us. Our Higher Power works through people who love us back to life.

With time, we begin returning this care and love to others. We feel this warm love flow right through us and out to others. We're kind without trying to be. We smile at others for no reason. We comfort those who hurt just by holding them.

Prayer for the Day

Higher Power, use me to make Your love real to someone today.

Action for the Day

Fear sometimes keeps me from loving. I'll list three things I'm afraid will happen if I'm "too loving." I'll share these fears with my sponsor.

*Archie doesn't know how to
worry without getting
upset.*
— *Edith Bunker*

Most of us are like Edith's television husband, Archie. When we worry, we get upset. Problems seem too big for us. We get afraid. We feel powerless.

What does the program tell us to do when we feel powerless and our life is upset? We look at the problem honestly. Then we ask our Higher Power to help us with the problem. We take it One Day at a Time. We believe our Higher Power will take care of us and help us.

We'll have problems. That's life! But we can get through them with care and support. We don't have to get crazy. We don't have to make things worse. We can be kind to ourselves and live through problems just fine—with our Higher Power's help.

Prayer for the Day

Higher Power, help me do what I can today about my problems. Help me stop worrying.

Action for the Day

If I have a problem today, I'll do what I can—and I'll leave the outcome to my Higher Power.

*I never loved another
person the way I loved
myself.*

— Mae West

This sums up how we used to live. We were in love with ourselves. We had to be on center stage. Our self-will ran riot.

Recovery pulls us out of that world. We learn to focus on others. We learn to reach out to them with love. This is the best way to love ourselves.

This doesn't mean that we live our lives through others. It means we invite others into our lives. It also means we ask to be invited into their lives. Recovery breaks down our self-will. It makes room for others in our lives.

Prayer for the Day
Higher Power, I give You my self-will. I know You'll do better with it than me.

Action for the Day
I'll list three ways my self-will has messed up my life. How am I doing at turning over these things to my Higher Power?

*Every saint has a past and
every sinner has a future.*
— *Oscar Wilde*

We all change. We learn, and change, and grow. We once made alcohol or other drugs our Higher Power. Perhaps we had other higher powers too—like money, gambling, food, or sex. But, it's never too late to be in touch with a true Higher Power. Each day we do this, we're saints. Each day we follow a false higher power, we aren't.

Prayer for the Day

Higher Power, help me put my life and will in Your hands today. Help me be a saint, just for today.

Action for the Day

How have my ideas about saints and sinners changed since I got into a Twelve Step program? I'll talk with my sponsor about it today.

Money costs too much.
— *Ross MacDonald*

Many people are poor and really need money to live better lives. But we're in trouble if we think money will solve all our problems. If money solved all problems, all rich people would be happy.

Consider this: A man talks about his shortcomings in a Twelve Step meeting. He says his main shortcoming is to think being happy means having enough money. But then he says that he has over a million dollars!

This man is lucky—not because he has money, but because he knows greed is a shortcoming. He knows he has a spiritual problem. He doesn't need money; he needs faith in a Higher Power.

Prayer for the Day

Higher Power, help me to really believe I'll be given what I need. This will free me to get on with life.

Action for the Day

Today, I'll read over the promises of the program. They are found at the bottom of page 83 and at the top of page 84 in the Big Book, *Alcoholics Anonymous*, Third Edition.

Skill to do comes of doing.
— Ralph Waldo Emerson

Often, we just want to sit and do nothing. And why not? We go to meetings, work the Twelve Steps, read, make new friends. All this takes energy and means taking risks. Haven't we earned the right to just sit and take a break from it all?

No! In the past, we avoided life. Now we're becoming people of action. We take risks. We're becoming people who get involved in life. We practice caring about people and caring about ourselves. At times, we may complain, but we do what is needed to stay sober. We gain skills by doing.

Why? We do it to save our lives. How? By trusting. We now trust that our Higher Power and friends will be there for us. They will help us push past our fears. As we *practice* daily how to stay sober, our skills grow.

Prayer for the Day
Higher Power, Yours is a spirit of action. Allow me to become skilled at being active.

Action for the Day
Today, I'll work at being active and alive. Maybe I'll start a new friendship or try a new meeting.

Speak when you're angry
and you'll make the best
speech you'll ever regret.
— Lawrence J. Peter

When we used alcohol or other drugs, most of us were hotheads. We thought we were right. If we were proven wrong, we may have made life hell for everyone. People knew enough to stay away from us.

In recovery, things will still go badly at times. We'll get hurt. And we'll get angry. But now, our anger no longer controls us. We also turn over our anger to our Higher Power. In our groups, we talk about what makes us angry. Then we leave the anger behind when the meeting is over. We find that being at peace is now more important than getting even.

Prayer for the Day

Higher Power, when I'm angry, help me slow down. Help me remember it's okay to be angry, but it's not okay to abuse people.

Action for the Day

I will remember a time when I turned anger into rage and hurt someone. I will also remember a time I was angry in a respectful way.

*You can make more friends
in two months by becoming
interested in other people
than you can in two years
of trying to get other people
interested in you.*
— *Dale Carnegie*

We wanted friends, but our addiction wanted all our attention. We had no time to be close to others.

Well, stand aside, addiction! The program has taught us that others are important. Our purpose is to help others. People have become what's important to us.

Now we *listen* to others. We help them do what *they* want to do, not what *we* want them to do. We help people instead of use them. Friendship is now a way of life. And another promise of the program becomes a part of us.

Prayer for the Day

Higher Power, help me to know that I'm here to help others, not just myself. Through others, I find myself.

Today's Action

Today I'll help someone in the way he or she wants to be helped.

*With each sunrise, we start
anew.*
— *Anonymous*

Like a tree, our life depends on new growth. There are many ways to bring new ideas and growth into our lives. We can attend Twelve Step retreats. We can study books and tapes on spirituality. We can attend different Twelve Step meetings.

But our spiritual newness may not just come from the Twelve Steps. We can do volunteer work or be active in other types of groups. We need to invite new ideas into our lives. We need to stay open to change. It doesn't matter what renews our spiritual growth. What matters is that we keep our spiritual lives fresh and growing.

Prayer for the Day

Higher Power, spring is one of the four seasons. Help me feel like spring. Help me to be strong but not stuck. Help me be firm yet open to spiritual growth.

Action for the Day

Today I'll try to do something new. When I get stuck or stubborn, I'll see that it's due to my fear of trying new ideas.

Youth is happy because it has the ability to see beauty. Anyone who keeps the ability to see beauty never grows old.
— *Franz Kafka*

Our addiction closed our eyes to the beauty of the world. The longer our disease went on, the uglier we felt and acted. We looked at honesty as an enemy, not as a friend.

In recovery, we start over. As time goes on, we work to stay young in the program. We need to be beginners. We need the eyes of a child to stay sober. We might think we know how to stay sober. This thinking can be full of danger. Instead, we need to see staying sober as a gift. It's a gift that's given one day at a time. We need to stay open to the beauty of the Twelve Steps and the gifts they hold.

Prayer for the Day

Higher Power, help me stay a beginner in this program. Have me see the beauty of the world. My addiction made me old. Help me regain my youth.

Today's Action

Today I'll study the children I meet. I'll learn much from their gentle beauty.

*If anything, we have
tended to be people who
wanted it all now. To hope
is not to demand.*
                        — *On Hope*

Maybe we were a bit demanding. Maybe we were a bit impatient. Maybe that's why we had such little hope.

Hope is believing good will come, even in bad times. Hope is knowing that "this, too, shall pass." Hope is knowing that no matter how afraid we are, God will be with us. Hope is knowing we never have to be alone again. It is knowing that time is on our side. Hope is giving up control. Hope is knowing we never had control in the first place. Hope is believing in ourselves. Hope is what our program is all about.

Prayer for the Day

Higher Power, in our program we share our experiences, our strengths, and our hopes. Thank you for giving all three of these to me to share.

Action for the Day

I will share my hope for the future with myself, my Higher Power, and my friends. I also will share this with someone who has lost hope.

> *Love your enemy—it will*
> *drive him nuts.*
> — *Eleanor Doan*

Love your enemy. It's a lot easier on you! Hating someone takes so much time and energy.

Loving your enemy means, instead of trying to get even, you let your Higher Power handle that person. Of course, loving your enemy is also hard. It means giving up control. It means giving up self-will. We addicts naturally want to control things and people.

This is where we turn to our program for help. We learn to love our enemies, not for some grand reason. We simply do it because hate can cause us to use alcohol or other drugs again.

Prayer for the Day

Higher Power, watch over my family, friends, and my enemies. Take from me my desire to control. Take from me *all* reasons to get high.

Action for the Day

Today, I'll list all of my enemies. I'll say each of their names, and then I'll read the Third Step out loud.

*The artist who aims at
perfection in everything
achieves it in nothing.*
— *Eugene Delacroix*

Trying to be perfect puts distance between us and our Higher Power. Trying to be perfect shows we're ashamed of being human. In recovery, we accept that we're human. We try to be the best *human* we can be.

We used to get high to feel powerful and god-like. But God is not just power. God is also gentleness. Gentleness and love are the power we look for in recovery. We give up trying to be perfect. We work to be human. We work to know the loving, gentle side of ourselves and our Higher Power. Remember, if we try to be a god, we'll fail. If we try to be human, we'll win.

Prayer for the Day

Higher Power, help me give up trying to be perfect. Help me always keep in mind that I'm human—which means, I'm not perfect.

Action for the Day

Part of being human is making mistakes. Today, I'll see my mistakes as chances to learn.

*I'm gonna die with my
boots on.*

— *Gene Autry*

Most of us don't like to think about death. But it's a sure thing, and we have to face it. First, we face the deaths of people around us. Then, some day, we'll face our own.

Most of us want to go quickly—"with our boots on"—when we die. We're afraid of illness, of pain, of being helpless. We're afraid of needing other people.

But being in the program teaches us it's okay to need other people. It's nice to accept their care and love for us. And no matter how we die, our trust in our Higher Power lets us face our fears with courage.

Prayer for the Day

Higher Power, help me live fully today. Help me put my life in Your hands.

Action for the Day

Is there anything I need to do before I die? Can I do it today? If I can, I will.

*The secret of success is
constancy of purpose.*
— *Benjamin Disraeli*

In Twelve Step meetings, we don't talk about counseling, treatment centers, or non-program reading. Many of us have been helped in these ways, but we shouldn't confuse them with Twelve Step programs.

We must keep our Twelve Step programs pure, no matter what is in style among counselors or at treatment centers, or what the latest books say. Certainly, we should use these sources if they help us, but not in our program meetings. There, we must stick to the basics that have helped addicts recover all over the world for many years. Steps, traditions, meetings, sponsorship—these things work, no matter what is in style.

Prayer for the Day
Higher Power, let me be there to help an addict in need, by sharing my Twelve Step program.

Action for the Day
I will help out today by being a sponsor or by calling a new group member, just to say hello.

*God is not a cosmic
bellboy.*
  — Harry Emerson Fosdick

We have to laugh when we look back at the times we treated God like our servant. Who did we think we were, ordering God to do something for us? But we got away with it. God even did some of the things we asked.

Now we know that our Higher Power is not a servant. As we work the Steps, we know we don't give orders to our Higher Power. We don't expect God to work miracles every time we'd like one. We're asking our Higher Power to lead us. After all, who knows what is best for us—our Higher Power or us?

Our Higher Power has many wonderful gifts for us. Our Higher Power will show us goals, help us live in love and joy, and give us strength.

Prayer for the Day

Higher Power, show me ways to help others as You've helped me. I'm grateful that You love me and help me.

Action for the Day

Today, I'll make a list of times my Higher Power has helped me out of trouble.

Whatever is in the heart
will come up to the tongue.
— Persian proverb

During our illness, we wouldn't let people get close to us. We spoke much of what was in our heart. And much of what filled our heart was sadness, anger, and hopelessness. Those who wanted to be close to us heard what was in our heart. In short, we had become our illness.

Recovery is about changing what's in our heart. We open our heart to the program and to its healing. We open our heart up to our Higher Power.

The first three Steps are about opening our hearts. They're about honesty and needing others. They're about turning our will and our lives over to a Higher Power. If you're wondering where you are with these Steps, listen to the words you speak.

Prayer for the Day
Higher Power, keep my heart open to the first three Steps.

Action for the Day
Today, I'll work at really listening to what I have to say.

*Spirituality is...the
awareness that survival is
a savage fight between you
and yourself.*

— Lisa S.

As recovering people, we're getting stronger each day. We go to meetings to learn how to be better people. But we also go to remind ourselves of the beast inside us—our addiction. This beast is waiting for us to slip—to go back to our addiction—so it can regain control.

Thus, it's wise to learn all we can about our disease. That's why it's important to do a good job on our Fourth Step. When we work Step Four, we learn how our addiction acts, thinks, and feels. With the help of our program, we can quiet the beast, One Day at a Time.

Prayer for the Day
Higher Power, I'm fighting for my life. Thanks to You, I'm winning today and my life is free.

Action for the Day
I'll talk to a friend about my addiction, the beast inside me. I'll do this so it will have less power over me.

*You grow up the day you
have your first real laugh
at yourself.*
— *Ethel Barrymore*

There was a time when we wouldn't let anyone laugh at us—even ourselves. We had too much shame. We had too much pain. We took the world too seriously. If we laughed, it was at others—not at ourselves.

Over time, real and honest laughter returns to us. Laughter is a way of accepting ourselves as human. To be human means we can make mistakes. It means we can lighten up. It also means growing up. And growing up means being happy with *all* of who we are—even parts of us that may seem odd or funny. If we can't laugh at ourselves, we shut ourselves off from the world. We shut ourselves off from the parts of us we need to accept. Am I willing to accept the fact that I'm human?

Prayer for the Day
Higher Power, You made laughter. Help me use it to make my life easier. Help me accept *all* of me.

Today's Action
Today, I'll share with someone close to me a funny mistake I've made.

April

*M*ade a searching
and fearless moral
inventory of ourselves.

— *Step Four*
from Alcoholics
Anonymous

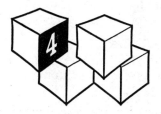

*Made a searching and
fearless moral inventory of
ourselves.*
— *Step Four of Alcoholics
Anonymous*

We avoid the Fourth Step. We put it off. We're scared of what we will find inside of us. We may find out we're mean, angry, selfish, afraid. We might see how badly we've acted to others, to ourselves. We have power to hurt, and we've used it. We all have these things inside of us.

We also have love, trust, faith, and hope. We love art, music, nature, or sports. We have power to heal, and we have used it too.

The Fourth Step helps us to know our inner power. As we learn about our own power, we can use it carefully, on purpose, to do good.

Prayer for the Day

Higher Power, help me use my power to do Your will. Let Your power work through me too.

Action for the Day

Today I'll watch my own actions and words. I'll see how my power affects others. I'll talk about this with my sponsor.

To know all things is not permitted.

— *Horace*

In recovery, we give up trying to be perfect. We give up trying to know everything. We work at coming to know and accept our shortcomings. In Steps Four and Five, we look at our good points and our bad points. In Step Six, we become ready to have our Higher Power remove our "defects of character." Then in Step Seven we ask our Higher Power to remove our "shortcomings."

Recovery is about coming to accept that we're not perfect. We admit that trying to be perfect got in the way of being useful to ourselves, our Higher Power, and those around us. Pretending to be perfect doesn't allow us to be real. It's also boring and no fun—you never get to mess up.

Prayer for the Day

Higher Power, You will let me know what I need to know. Allow me to claim my mistakes and shortcomings.

Action for the Day

I will work at being okay today. Not perfect, just okay.

*Rest is the guardian of
health.*
— *Melba Colgrove*

Now that we're sober, we're feeling better than we have in years. We're busy too. We attend meetings and visit friends. We have work, school, families, and homes to keep up with.

It's easy to forget to rest. We forget that our bodies and minds need time off. We need plenty of sleep each night. And we need a lazy weekend now and then to let our bodies recover from the *go, go, go* of daily life.

Prayer for the Day

Higher Power, help me listen to my body. Remind me to slow down and rest now and then.

Action for the Day

How much have I rested lately? Have I gotten enough sleep each night? What can I do in the next two days to rest my body, mind, and spirit?

*Pray without resentment in
your heart.*
— The Little Red Book

Resentment is anger that we don't want to
turn over to our Higher Power. Sometimes, we
want to keep our anger. Maybe we want to
"get even." It's hard to be spiritual and full
of anger at the same time. When we hold on
to anger, it turns into self-will.

We all get angry from time to time. This is
normal. But we now have a program to help
us let go of anger. We also know that stored-
up anger can drive us back to alcohol and
other drugs. Instead of trying to "get even,"
let's work at keeping anger out of our hearts.

Prayer for the Day

I pray without anger in my heart. Higher Power,
I give You my anger. Have me work for justice, instead of acting like a judge.

Action for the Day

I'll list any resentments I now have. I'll talk about
them at my next meeting. This is the best way to
turn resentments over to my Higher Power.

Go outside, to the fields,
enjoy nature and the
sunshine, go out and try to
recapture happiness in
yourself and in God.
　　　　　— *Anne Frank*

Many of us first looked at the joy and beauty of the program with caution. It was different from our addictive joy. Was it to be trusted?

When we started working the Steps, we found inner joy and beauty. As we let go and gave in to the program, we found more happiness. We found joy in ourselves, our friends, our Higher Power, and those around us. Our self-pity changed to self-respect. We were truly out in the sunshine. We were no longer lost in misery. We now know how to walk through misery to find joy.

Prayer for the Day

May I become better friends with my self. Higher Power, let me see the world through Your innocent, yet wise and loving eyes.

Today's Action

Today I'll work to make my life and the lives of others more joyful. I'll greet myself and others with much joy.

To know the road ahead,
ask those coming back.
    — Chinese proverb

We're going down a new road—in our recovery and in our lives. We don't know the road. We only know we're on the right one, because our Higher Power led us here.

We ask for help from those who already know the road. We ask our sponsor, "How far is it until I get done feeling guilty?" "How far to self-love?" "How bumpy is the road when I'm at Step Four?"

We need the help of people who have been in the program. They tell us where to slow down because this part of the trip is beautiful.

Someday, maybe today, we too will be called on to guide others.

Prayer for the Day

Higher Power, You've put me on this road. You've also put others on this road. Let them be my guides. Let my guides become my friends.

Action for the Day

Today, I'll find someone who has been in the program two or more years longer than me. I'll ask that person what the road ahead is like.

Better bend than break.
— Scottish proverb

At times, we need to take a stand. But there will be more times when we'll need to bend. Bending means listening to other opinions. Often, we just react instead of listening. Bending means remembering what's really important. Often, we get stubborn just to prove a point. Bending means knowing that, most often, the relationship is more important than the point we want to prove.

Bending is about letting go. Often, what we need to let go of is our self-will. If we live only by self-will, we'll eventually break. Self-will is as fragile as fine china. We need to be more like Tupperware than fine china—we'll last longer and be invited to dinner more often.

Prayer for the Day

Higher Power, You made the trees. They stand, but they also bend, especially when they're young and growing.

Action for the Day

I'll list three times in my life where knowing how to bend would've been helpful.

*It's a simple formula: "Do
your best and somebody
might like it."*
— *Dorothy Baker*

Our program is a selfish program. It tells us
to let go of what others think. We're staying
sober for ourselves, not for anyone else. Our
body and our spirit are at stake. And we know
what we need to do to stay sober. If we feel
shaky about going to a party, we don't go—
no matter who gets upset. If our job makes
it hard to stay sober, we get a different one—
no matter who gets upset. It's simple.

We must take good care of ourselves before
we can be good to others. In doing this, we
learn how to be a friend, a good parent, a good
spouse. We have to care for ourselves to have
good relationships. Do I believe it's okay to be
selfish when it comes to my program?

Prayer for the Day

Higher Power, help me do what is best for my
recovery, no matter what others think.

Action for the Day

I will remind myself that staying sober is simple.
I don't use chemicals. And I work the program.

*The best thing about the
future is that it comes only
one day at a time.*
— Abraham Lincoln

Abraham Lincoln did great things for the
United States. He took life One Day at a Time.
He broke the future into manageable pieces.
We can do the same. We can live in the
present and focus on the task at hand.
Spirituality comes when we focus this way.
When we stay in the present we find choice.
And we worry less about the future.

Still, we must have goals. We must plan for
our future. Goals and plans help us give more
credit to the present than to the future. And
when we feel good about the present, we feel
good about the future.

Prayer for the Day

Higher Power, help me focus. Help me keep my
energy in the present. Have me live life One Day
at a Time.

Action for the Day

When I find myself drifting into the future, I'll
work at bringing myself back to the present.

*You cannot prevent the
birds of sadness from
passing over your head,
but you can prevent their
making nests in your hair.*
— *Chinese proverb*

Life is full of feelings. We can be happy, sad,
mad, scared. These feelings can come and go
quickly. Or we may hang on to them. As
recovering addicts, we used to hang on to feelings that made us feel bad. We let them make
"nests" in our hair. We used our feelings as
an excuse to drink or use other drugs.

Now we're learning to hang on to our good
feelings. We can let go of anger, hurt, and fear
We can shoo away the birds of sadness and
welcome the birds of happiness.

Prayer for the Day
Higher Power, help me become a "bird watcher."
Help me learn from my feelings. And help me let
go of the bad ones so I can be happy.

Action for the Day
If I need to get rid of the sadness or anger that
I'm hanging on to, I'll get help from my sponsor,
a counselor, or a clergyperson.

Fools, through false shame,
conceal their open wounds.
  — Horace

Many of us, as children, were taught to hide our pain, to act as if we had none. We looked for ways to hide our pain. Alcohol and other drugs helped us do this. But the pain always returned. We were ashamed that we hurt. We thought we were the only ones who hurt so badly. And, worst of all, we thought our pain meant we were bad people.

Ours is a program of honesty. As we live life, there will be troubles, and there will be pain. But now we know that we don't try to hide it. If we hide our wounds, they will not heal. We will listen to others' pains and ask them to listen to ours. This will help us continue our journey in recovery.

Prayer for the Day
God, help me be honest about my pain. Help me see pain not as a personal defect, but as a part of life.

Action for the Day
I'll share my pain with a friend, a family member, my group, or sponsor. I'll ask them to do the same with me. I'll think of pain as part of life.

> *Life I love you, all is*
> *groovy.*
> — *Paul Simon*

Working the Twelve Steps is more than recovery from alcohol or other drug addiction. It's also about how to enjoy life.

Our illness pulled us toward death. Our spirits were dying, and maybe even our bodies were dying. Now our spirits are coming to life. We feel more alive than ever before. Our feelings are coming alive. We feel hope and faith, love and joy, and even hurt and fear. We notice the sunshine as well as the clouds. We know life needs both sunshine and rain, both joy and pain. We are alive!

Prayer for the Day

Higher Power, help me let go of my fears and enjoy life. I haven't always known how to enjoy life, but You can teach me. All life is from You, so teach me to be free in Your light and love.

Today's Action

Right now, I can think of at least three things in life that make me feel like sunshine. What are they?

*No labor, however humble,
is dishonoring.*
— *The Talmud*

Work is good for our hearts. Work is good for our minds. It can give us something to focus on besides ourselves. Labor doesn't just mean having a job. It may mean planting a garden or helping a friend. It certainly means working our program. Hopefully, it's a labor of love.

We can get in trouble if we have too much time on our hands. We can turn it into mischief or self-pity. We can get bored. Being bored is a matter of choice. We'll never be bored if we ask ourselves, "How can I make this world a better place?" We can then turn our answers into action.

Prayer for the Day

Higher Power, teach me to use my time wisely. Help me be well-balanced between labor and fun. I need both.

Action for the Day

I'll list five ways that labor and fun can help me get closer to my Higher Power. And I'll look for people and things to fill my time in positive ways.

It is enough that I am of
value to somebody today.
— Hugh Prather

Even in recovery, we addicts often feel we
are not enough. Maybe it's leftover shame
from our using days. But we *are* enough. We
are of great value. We all need each other to
stay sober.

Each of us needs other recovering people
to help us remember the hell of addiction. We
can forget how bad it was, but telling our
stories makes us remember. When you feel
you don't want to stay sober for yourself, then
stay sober for your brothers and sisters in the
program. They need you. You're their recovery, as they're yours. There may be days you
don't feel glad to be sober. But your friends
in this fellowship are glad you're sober. They
thank-you for your sobriety.

Prayer for the Day
Higher Power, may Your will, not mine, be done.

Action for the Day
I'll stop and think of all the people I'm glad for.
I'll start telling them today.

That day is lost on which
one has not laughed.
            — French proverb

For a long time, we didn't really laugh. It's surprising when we think about it: we hadn't really laughed for so long. . .we almost forgot how good we could feel. It feels so good to laugh again!

Now, our spirits come more alive each day. Now, we feel what alcohol and other drugs stuffed deep inside us. Pain, fear, and anger come up. But so do happiness and joy, thankfulness and a sense of humor. In early recovery, we work through the hard feelings. As we grow in the program, we have more and more room for happiness.

Prayer for the Day
Higher Power, wake me up to the joy and laughter that today holds for me. Don't let me miss it!

Action for the Day
Today, I'll spread some laughter. I will learn a joke and tell it to three people.

No human creature can
give orders to love.
— *George Sand*

If we're trying to get others to love us, all we're really doing is trying to be in control. Trying to control others can be a powerful drug. Remember, we can't control others. We can't *make* others love us. Our Higher Power has control, not us.

So, what do we need to do? Turn things over to our Higher Power and just be ourselves.

Sure, it can scare us to just be ourselves. The truth is, not everyone will love us. But if we're honest about who we are, others will respect us. We'll like ourselves better. And we'll have a better chance of loving others and being loved.

Prayer for the Day

I pray to have my need for control lifted from me. I pray to be rid of self-will.

Action for the Day

Today, I'll list five ways my self-will—my need to control—has gotten me in trouble.

We create revolution by
living it.
> — Jerry Rubin

There's a lot wrong in the world—child abuse, homeless and hungry people, pollution. Our old way of dealing with these troubles was to break the rules or to "drop out" by using chemicals.

Now we have a new way to change the world. We're changing ourselves. One Day at a Time, we're acting like the caring, responsible people we want to be. We use the ideas of the program in our lives.

We're kinder. We're more honest. We stand up for ourselves and for others who need our help. What if the whole world started working the Steps? What a wonderful world this would be!

Prayer for the Day

Higher Power, please work through me today. Help me make the world a little better place.

Action for the Day

I'll list one thing that bothers me about the world today. How can using the ideas of the program help solve that problem? Remember, the program tells us to look at our *own* behavior.

Patience is needed with everyone, but first of all with ourselves.
— *St. Francis de Sales*

How do you treat yourself? Do you talk to yourself with a kind and loving voice? We can't be kind and loving to others until we learn to be kind and loving with ourselves. To live this way, we must give ourselves the gift of patience.

Let's practice patience with ourselves daily. Practice talking to yourself in a kind, loving voice. Over time, this will become your every-day voice. Your voice will be that of a loving parent who helps a child with a new task. Your Higher Power is willing to be patient with you. Give yourself the same gift.

Prayer for the Day

Higher Power, I pray that I'll treat myself and others with the same loving patience You've shown me.

Action for the Day

I will listen to how I talk to myself. I will practice talking to myself with a kind, loving, and patient voice.

*We give thanks for
unknown blessings already
on their way.*
— Sacred ritual chant

Good things keep happening to us. We are sober. We can think clearly. We can see progress on how we handle our problems. We have friends. We have love. We have hope.

We are starting to love ourselves. We are starting to feel joy. Our fears are getting smaller. We are starting to trust our new way of life. Our new life brings good things to us. It brings blessings every day. We are beginning to expect them. But we're still surprised at how good life can be. What a difference from the days before we entered our program!

Prayer for the Day

Higher Power, thank-you for the blessings You keep on giving me. And thanks for whatever today will bring.

Action for the Day

One way to give thanks for my blessings is to share them with others. How can I share my recovery today?

*A great obstacle to
happiness is to expect too
much happiness.*
— *Fontenelle*

Our disease is sometimes called the disease
of "always wanting more." We pushed ourselves to get as much pleasure as we could.
If one was good, two was better. We didn't see
that what we were lacking was faith.

At times, in recovery, we still crave "more."
We must pay attention to these cravings.
When we have a craving, maybe we're scared,
and our Higher Power is trying to tell us that,
if we have faith, we'll be taken care of. Perhaps
our Higher Power just has a message of love
for us. All we need to do is listen. It may be
that this is the only "more" we really need.

Prayer for the Day

I pray to see my cravings as spiritual needs. I
pray to turn to my Higher Power instead of to alcohol or other drugs.

Action for the Day

Today, I'll think about how much recovery has
given me. I will share this with a friend and with
my Higher Power.

*One of the most important
parts of the A.A. program
is to give our drink problem
to God honestly and fully...*
— Twenty-Four Hours a Day,
   March 1

We don't *handle* our drinking or other drug problem. We don't *take care* of this problem by ourselves. We *turn* our problem over to *God* as we understand Him. We need to be very clear about this. *We can't handle our drinking or other drug problem!* Our Higher Power keeps us sober through the Steps and the fellowship of the program.

Our job is to hand over our problem to our Higher Power. We do this daily by acting like sober people.

Prayer for the Day
Higher Power, I know I can't handle drinking and using other drugs. I turn my problem over to you. Please take from me the urge to drink or use.

Action for the Day
Today, I'll remember why I *can't* handle or take care of my problem with alcohol or other drugs. And I'll remember why my Higher Power *can.*

*One meets his destiny often
on the road one takes to
avoid it.*

— *French proverb*

None of us, perhaps, ever thought we'd end up in recovery. But we were working at joining recovery years before we got here! Maybe recovery was our fate from the day we first took a drink or a pill. Others around us could see the writing on the wall, but we couldn't. We were too busy trying to avoid pain.

Alcoholism and other drug abuse have to do with us trying to find spiritual wholeness— the kind of spiritual wholeness we're finding now. . .in recovery. So, let's welcome recovery into our lives. We have found our spiritual home.

Prayer for the Day

Higher Power, I got lost because I acted like I knew the way to a good life. You lead the way. Thank-you for putting me on the right track.

Action for the Day

Today, I'll think about why it's my fate to be in recovery. I will list ways that I try to avoid my fate.

*When people talk, listen
completely. Most people
never listen.*
— *Ernest Hemingway*

It's hard to listen in a complete way. Often we listen, but we're still thinking about ourselves. We wonder, "How do their words relate to me? Do I have anything to add?" Often, fear is behind these questions. We fear saying the wrong thing. We fear looking stupid.

Good listeners know how to let go. They let go of their fears. To listen completely, we step outside ourselves, and we're totally there for someone else. Sometimes we listen for only a few moments. Sometimes we don't even agree with the people we're listening to. But we let them know that they count. What a gift we give when we listen in a complete way!

Prayer for the Day

Higher Power, teach me to listen in a complete way. Teach me to step outside myself and be there for others.

Action for the Day

Today, I'll *listen* to what the person says.

*The hardest thing to learn
in life is which bridge to
cross and which bridge to
burn.*
— David Russell

Making big decisions is like crossing bridges. Sometimes, these decisions change our lives. We find that turning back will be very hard. This is why we have to be very careful when we decide to burn bridges.

When we decide to make changes, we act carefully. We don't want to make decisions out of anger or envy. Instead, we can think about what we want and how our program can help us make wise decisions.

Prayer for the Day

Higher Power, help me cross those bridges that are on my path.

Action for the Day

What do I really want in life? What decisions do I need to make to get there?

*You're never too old to
grow up.*
                    — Shirley Conran

Some of us have spent many years trying
not to grow up. As children, we watched the
adults around us. They may not have seemed
happy. "Is life all hard work for grown-ups?"
we wondered.

No, it's not all hard work. There are lots of
good things about growing up. We can take
charge of our life. We can learn to take care
of ourselves. We can learn to share our feelings with good friends. We can make our
world safe enough for us to express feelings
again. We can learn how to love others. We *do*
have choices.

Prayer for the Day
Higher Power, help me grow up into a happy,
grateful adult.

Action for the Day
There are happy grown-ups. I'll find one to be
my sponsor.

*Too many people miss the
silver lining because
they're expecting gold.*
— *Maurice Setter*

Silver shines just as bright as gold does. So often we forget this. So often we push, push, push. We forget to live for the moment. Trying too hard can be a defect of character. It can be a way we avoid life.

Gratitude, being thankful, is a key part of recovery. Not just gratitude for getting our self-respect back. Not just gratitude for having a Higher Power. But gratitude for the moment. We're alive again. Let's see each moment as a time to explore life.

Prayer for the Day
Higher Power, thanks for helping me to enjoy each moment. I have gratitude for being alive.

Action for the Day
I'll list ten gifts of recovery for which I have gratitude.

*I noticed my hopelessness
was because I had lost my
freedom of choice.*
                    — AA member

By doing a Fourth Step, we start to see ourselves more clearly. We see how we've acted
against ourselves. Soon, we hear a little voice
inside telling us to *stop* before we act. "Are
you sure you want to say or do that?" the
little voice asks. Then we make a choice: we
do something the same old way, or we try a
new way.

One part of us will always want to do things
the old, sick way. This is natural. But we're
getting stronger every day. Our spirit wants
to learn new ways so we can be honest and
loving. Sometimes we don't know how. But
we still have a choice. We can ask for help.

Prayer for the Day

Higher Power, help me listen to the little voice
inside that helps me see that I have choices.

Action for the Day

Today, I'll make a choice between old ways and
new ways of acting. I will call my sponsor this evening to talk about my choices.

*Unless I accept my faults I
will most certainly doubt
my virtues.*
— *Hugh Prather*

Before recovery, we saw only a blurry picture of ourselves, like we were looking through an out-of-focus camera lens. We couldn't see the good in ourselves because we wouldn't look close enough.

Step Four helps us look more closely. We see a clear picture of ourselves, with our good points and our faults. We don't like everything we see. But we can't change until we accept ourselves as we are. Then we can start getting ready to change.

Prayer for the Day
Higher Power, help me see the good in me and love myself.

Action for the Day
Today, I'll make a list of four of my good points and four of my faults. Am I getting ready to have my Higher Power remove these defects of character?

*I'm as pure as the driven
slush.*
> — *Tallulah Bankhead*

The Steps are filled with words and phrases like *shortcomings, exact nature of our wrongs, persons we had harmed,* and *when we were wrong.* The Steps help us accept *all* parts of who we are.

Our program asks us to share these parts of ourselves with others. We heal by doing this. It's hard to talk about how wrong we can be, but we must. It's part of how we recover. Remember, all of us have bad points. At times, we all act like jerks. When we can talk about our mistakes, we end up having less shame inside of us.

Prayer for the Day
Higher Power, help me to love and accept myself—as You love and accept me. Give me the courage to share *all* my secret wrongs.

Action for the Day
Today, I'll review my Fourth Step. If I haven't done this Step, I'll start today.

*When you want to be
something, it means you
really love it.*
— *Andy Warhol*

At times, we turned to chemicals because we couldn't love ourselves. Our addiction gave a promise of relief, but it gave us self-hate. We wanted to love, but couldn't.

What is it we really love? Where should we put our energy? In raising children? In creating art? In helping addicts who still suffer? There's much in this world that needs our love. We can be many things in our lives. Let's be people we believe in. Let's be people we're proud of. Let's be people we can love.

Prayer for the Day

Higher Power, help me know myself through my inventories. My skills, talents, values, and my loves must be clear to me so I can use them to do Your will.

Today's Action

Today I'll think about what I'd really love to do through my work.

*A*dmitted to God,
to ourselves, and to
another human being the
exact nature of our wrongs.

— *Step Five*
from Alcoholics
Anonymous

*Admitted to God, to
ourselves, and to another
human being the exact
nature of our wrongs.*
— *Step Five*

Step Five can be scary. We're to take the
wrongs we listed in our Fourth Step and share
them with God, ourselves, and another person.
We may look for an easier, softer way. But
Step Five stops us.

We're to share the *exact* nature of our
wrongs. Why? So we can take a load off ourselves. So we won't use again. By totally sharing our past wrongs, we can belong once
more. We can heal. We can start to forgive ourselves. We become more humble. When you
share your Fifth Step, hold nothing back. You
deserve the peace this Step will bring you.

Prayer for the Day

Higher Power, give me courage to tell it all. Give
me courage to admit just how wrong I had become.

Action for the Day

Step Five teaches me that sharing is important.
I will find a friend and share my wrongs with that
friend. I will hold nothing back.

*Happiness is not a goal; it
is a by-product.*
— *Eleanor Roosevelt*

Most of us want to be happy. We just don't
know how. We aren't sure what happiness is.
We've learned the hard way that some things
we wanted didn't make us happy.

We're learning that happiness comes when
we live the way our Higher Power wants us to
live. That's when we're honest. When we do
our best work. When we are a true friend. We
make happiness; we don't find it.

Sometimes we don't even know we're happy.
We're too busy with our work, our recovery
program, our friends and family. We need to
slow down and know that when we do what
we need to, happiness comes.

Prayer for the Day

Higher Power, help me know that I'm most happy
when I listen to You and do Your will. You know
better than I do what will make me happy.

Today's Action

What parts of my program am I most happy
about? Today I'll think of these and enjoy myself.

When I have listened to my
mistakes, I have grown.
— Hugh Prather

Everyone makes mistakes. We all know that. So why is it so hard to admit our own? We seem to think we have to be perfect. We have a hard time looking at our mistakes. But our mistakes can be very good teachers.

Our Twelve Step program helps us learn and grow from our mistakes. In Step Four, half of our work is to think of our mistakes. In Step Five, we admit our mistakes to God, ourselves, and another person. We learn, we grow, and become whole. All by coming to know our mistakes. The gift of recovery is not being free of mistakes. Instead, we do the Steps to claim our mistakes and talk about them. We find the gift of recovery when we learn from our mistakes.

Prayer for the Day

Higher Power, help me to see my mistakes as chances to get to know myself better.

Today's Action

Today I'll talk to a friend about what my mistakes taught me. Today I'll feel less shame.

I am the greatest!
        — Muhammad Ali

We need to believe in ourselves. We're sober. We're honest. We're trustworthy. We're not making so many problems for other people anymore. We do our share. We can even help others sometimes.

We're glad that others help us. We thank our Higher Power every day. But we also give ourselves credit. We're working our program. We handle life as best we can. And as long as we ask our Higher Power to work through us, we *are* the greatest!

Prayer for the Day
Higher Power, help me feel proud of the changes in my life.

Action for the Day
Today, I'll talk with my sponsor about pride. What is good pride? What should I watch out for?

Forgiveness is all-powerful.
Forgiveness heals all ills.
— Catherine Ponder

We need to forgive so we can heal. Forgiveness means not wanting to get even. Forgiveness means letting go of self-will. Anger and hate are forms of self-will that take up room in our heart. Yet, a still, small voice inside of us wants to forgive. Just as others have forgiven us, we need to forgive them. When we forgive, we give our will to our Higher Power. When we forgive, we make room in our heart for our Higher Power. By giving up our anger and our hate, we let that still, small voice come through a little louder. This is how we heal. This is why forgiving is so powerful for us.

Prayer for the Day
Higher Power, help me let go of self-will. Help me forgive people.

Action for the Day
I will list any anger or hate I have. I will think about how this gets in my way, and I'll pray to have this removed.

*Anyone who follows a
middle course is called a
sage.*

— *Maimonides*

Much of the wisdom of our program is about how to live in the middle. We learn how to pause and think before we act. We ask, "What is the best way to handle this?" We look for the smooth part of the road.

Our actions tell us who we are. We listen to our actions, and we think about them. This listening and thinking takes time. This slows us down. It's good for us. It gives us time to talk with our Higher Power. After all, we want our actions to come from the new values our Higher Power has given us. Thus, over time we act and feel wiser. The wisdom of the program becomes part of who we are.

Prayer for the Day
I pray that I don't get caught up in the rush of the day. Higher Power, teach me to stop and think, to seek Your wisdom.

Action for the Day
Today, I'll set aside time to think, meditate, and be alone. I will listen to what's inside me.

*So live that you wouldn't be
ashamed to sell the family
parrot to the town gossip.*
— *Will Rogers*

Secrets help keep us sick. In our drinking
and using days, we did things we weren't
proud of. We lived in a secret world we were
ashamed of. This is part of the power of addiction. Our behavior and our secrets kept us
trapped.

Recovery offers us a way out of this secret
world. In our groups, we share our secrets,
and they lose their power over us. There may
be things we're too ashamed to talk about in
our groups. When we share these things in
our Fifth Step, they lose their power over us.

We have a new way of life that we're not
ashamed to talk about. When shame leaves,
pride enters our hearts. We know we're good
people!

Prayer for the Day

Higher Power, help me live a good life.

Action for the Day

Do I have any secrets that get in my way? Do I
need to do a Fifth Step? If so, I'll pick a date—today.

The only way to speak the
truth is to speak lovingly.
                    — Thoreau

Recovery teaches us to tell the truth. We must be honest if we want to save our lives. We must learn to speak with care—care for ourselves and for others.

To be honest means to speak in a fair and truthful way. To be honest and loving means learning *when* to speak, and *how* to speak, in a caring way. We can help others by honestly telling them what we think and feel and see—but only when we do this with love.

We must be careful when we speak. Speaking the truth is like using a very sharp knife—it can be used for good, or it can be used to hurt others. We should never handle it carelessly or use it to hurt someone.

Prayer for the Day

Higher Power, help me know the truth. Help me speak the truth to others with love.

Action for the Day

I'll make a list of three times I've hurt someone by being honest, but not with love. I'll also list three times I've helped someone by being truthful, with love.

The longer I live the more
beautiful life becomes.
— Frank Lloyd Wright

For many of us, life was a burden while using alcohol and other drugs. As our illness went on, life was more ugly. We grew further from our friends, family, and Higher Power.

In recovery, our eyes and hearts open a little more each day. We see the beauty that life holds. We now see that before recovery, we weren't living—we were dying. In recovery, we again may feel happy when we hold a baby. We again may feel joy when we see a sunset. This happens mainly because we've chosen to be with people who love life, people who've been given a second chance.

Once we've almost lost something important, it becomes more precious. We almost lost our lives. Now our lives are special.

Prayer for the Day

Higher Power, thank-you for a second chance. Thank-you for opening my eyes and heart. Give me the strength to keep them open.

Action for the Day

I'll list the most beautiful parts of my life. I'll open my heart today to the joy in store for me.

*As I grow older, I pay less
attention to what men say.
I just watch what they do.*
— Andrew Carnegie

Doing something with our lives, not just talking about it, is important. When we were sick with our addiction, what we did was drink or use other drugs. We only talked about what we wanted to do. Now that we are sober, we can really live our lives.

We've already done a lot. We've gotten help for our chemical dependency. We're facing the harm we did to our families. We've let other people into our lives.

Before recovery, we didn't have to tell people we were alcoholics and addicts. Our actions showed it, if people knew what to look for. Now we don't have to tell people we are recovering, because our actions will show it.

Prayer for the Day

Higher Power, let my actions show that I am getting better every day.

Action for the Day

Today, I'll let my actions speak louder than my words. I'll do one thing that I have been saying I want to do.

*An honest man's the
noblest work of God.*
— *Alexander Pope*

Step Five says, "Admitted to God, to ourselves, and to another human being the exact nature of our wrongs." When we did this Step, the person we admitted our wrongs to didn't run away or reject us. That person stuck with us. Chances are, we were told that we are quite human. And working Step Five helped us to see that we can change, now that we're sober.

The most important part of Step Five is the act of being totally honest about ourselves. Then we know that relationships—with our Higher Power, ourselves, and others—can be built. We have faced the truth. Now we know we never have to lie.

Prayer for the Day
Higher Power, I know no Fifth Step is perfect. Please help me be as honest as I can in doing my Fifth Step and at other times.

Action for the Day
If I've avoided doing a Fifth Step, I'll talk to my sponsor about it today.

*You can observe a lot just
by watching.*
— *Yogi Berra*

When we watch others, we learn how to "act as if." We watch a patient person, and then we "act as if" we're a patient person. The result? Over time, we'll become a patient person. We watch how good listeners listen, and we "act as if" we know how to listen. Then one day, we realize we're really listening! We watch people who have faith, and we "act as if" we have it. Then over time, we become spiritual people!

Prayer for the Day

Higher Power, help me find You in the people and events of my day.

Action for the Day

I will "act as if" my Higher Power is standing next to me all through the day.

*Hating people is like
burning down your own
house to get rid of a rat.*
— *Harry Emerson Fosdick*

Hate is like an illness. It steals our hope, our love, our relationships. Hate puts distance between people. Hate can give us a false sense of power. Do I use hate to make myself feel important?

Our program tells us to let go of hate. Hate and sobriety don't mix. Hate doesn't let us connect with our Higher Power.

Ours is a program of love and respect. We're taught that if someone treats us wrong, we still should be respectful in our response. Why? Because we're changed by our actions. If we act with hate, we become hateful. If we act in a respectful way, we become respectable.

Prayer for the Day

Hate is the drug of those who are afraid. Higher Power, help me to be free from hate today.

Action for the Day

It's self-centered to hate. Today, I'll read pages 60-62 of *Alcoholics Anonymous* (Third Edition) about being self-centered.

*Make yourself an honest
[person], and then you may
be sure that there is one
rascal less in the world.*
— *Thomas Carlyle*

Honesty does not mean saying all we think
or feel. Many of our thoughts and feelings are
only with us for a minute. They are not always
the truth. For example, saying to someone
you love, "I hate you!" in the middle of an
argument can destroy things.

Honesty means living by what is true to us.
Then we choose when and how to say things
to others. Think of honesty as the air we
breathe; it's what keeps us alive, but it can
get polluted and kill. It must be treated with
respect and care.

Prayer for the Day

Higher Power, help me know the power of
honesty. Help me speak it with care and respect.

Action for the Day

Before I speak today I'll ask myself: "Is this true?
Am I speaking because this needs to be said?"

*That day is lost on which
one has not laughed.*
— *French proverb*

For a long time, we didn't really laugh. It's surprising when we think about it: we hadn't really laughed for so long . . .we almost forgot how good we could feel. It feels so good to laugh again!

Now, our spirits come more alive each day. Now, we feel what alcohol and other drugs stuffed deep inside us. Pain, fear, and anger come up. But so do happiness and joy, thankfulness and a sense of humor. In early recovery, we work through the hard feelings. As we grow in the program, we have more and more room for happiness.

Prayer for the Day

Higher Power, wake me up to the joy and laughter that today holds for me. Don't let me miss it!

Action for the Day

Today, I'll spread some laughter. I will learn a joke and tell it to three people.

*The time to relax is when
you don't have time for it.*
— *Sydney J. Harris*

Relaxing is one of the little joys of life. We can learn to take time from our busy day to chat with a friend, take a hot bath, or spend a few moments sitting alone under a tree. The busier we are, the more we need to take time to relax.

When we rest, we stop fussing about the outside world. We find out how we're doing *inside*. While relaxing, we can best listen to our Higher Power. Our minds calm down. We put busy thoughts aside. Sometimes, we can almost hear our Higher Power say, "Stay quiet and listen! I have something to tell you!"

Prayer for the Day

Higher Power, remind me to relax. My spirit needs rest and quiet so I can hear You.

Action for the Day

Today, I'll list five ways I like to relax. I'll do one of them today.

*Each day provides its own
gifts.*
— *Ruth P. Freedman*

Spiritual growth is the greatest gift we can receive. And we earn it through taking risks. There is much risk involved in working the Steps: The risk of admitting that we're out of control. The risk of turning our will and our lives over to a Power greater than ourselves. The risk of letting go of character defects. The risk of making amends to people we've harmed. The risk of admitting our wrongs. The risk of telling our stories as we carry the message of hope. To grow spiritually, we need these adventures. These challenges. These risks.

Prayer for the Day
Higher Power, help me to take the risks that I need in order to grow.

Action for the Day
I will look at today as an adventure with my Higher Power. I will list the fears I'll need to let go of.

You cannot plan the future
by the past.
                    — Edmund Burke

We got tired of how we were living. We honestly looked at our life. We saw that alcohol and other drugs controlled our life. We met others who understood us. And we came to believe that a Power greater than ourselves could help us. We turned our will and our life over to this Power. In so doing, we learned that life doesn't take place in the past or in the future. We find life in the present. We find our program in the present.

Prayer for the Day
I pray that I'll leave the past in the past. I pray that I'll walk into each new moment with my Higher Power.

Action for the Day
The only time we revisit the past is when we tell our story. Today, I'll tell my story to someone. I'll tell what really happened. I'll tell what life is like now.

*The art of living is more like
wrestling than dancing.*
— *Marcus Aurelius*

The struggles of life teach us a lot. They challenge our beliefs. As we struggle, we come to believe that our friends, family, and Higher Power will be there for us in hard times. But we must do our part. We need to call and honestly let people know how we're doing. We need to pray and ask our Higher Power for help. If we do these things, we'll come to respect and learn from hard times.

Prayer for the Day

I pray for the wisdom to see that struggles are part of life. Higher Power, I pray for Your help in not taking struggles too personally.

Action for the Day

I'll list four times I've struggled and what I learned from each struggle. I'll share this with a friend.

*And if the blind lead the
blind, both shall fall into
the ditch.*
— Matt. 15:14

Twelve Step programs are sometimes called
self-help programs. But they're not really, because we all help each other. We don't stay
sober by ourselves. Sometimes we call Twelve
Step programs *peer programs.* And they are.
All of us are equal. No one is an expert. But
we need to be careful who we choose for a
sponsor. We each need to find someone who
has been sober longer than us. Someone who
understands the Steps. Someone who lives by
them. Someone we want to be like. We need
to stick with the winners.

Prayer for the Day

Higher Power, I know I'm like a blind person who
is just beginning to see. Help me follow the path
of those who see better than I do.

Action for the Day

Today, I'll list the people in my program I go to
for help. Am I sticking with the winners?

*Be not afraid of growing
slowly, be afraid only of
standing still.*
            — Chinese proverb

All of us are a little afraid of growth. We wonder how growth will change our lives. Who will we be? Will our friends still love us? Can't we grow up and get it over with? Why does it take so long?

All of us have a need to keep growing. There is no age when we're "all grown up" and all done learning. But we don't need to rush our growth. Like a child on a too-big bicycle, at times we'll find ourselves out of control. We'll tip over. We can grow at our own pace, but we must grow. We must make changes. Or else, like an athlete on a too-small bicycle, we won't get far. We'll tip over too!

Prayer for the Day

Higher Power, help me grow. And help me know my own strength as I grow.

Action for the Day

Am I fully using my strength, my mind, my talents? I will list one way that I can do this better.

*Showing up is 80 percent
of life.*
— *Woody Allen*

Life is full of things we don't want to do. Yet when *all* parts of us (mind, body, spirit) show up, things go okay. By being there, we can learn about ourselves and help others.

Showing up means we care about our program. It means we speak up at meetings. It means we care about our family, our friends, the world. It means we listen when a friend has a bad day. It means seeing ourselves in others. It means we talk to someone who bothers us. Showing up means we laugh when something seems funny. It means we cry when we feel sad. We're important, and we need to bring our mind, body, and spirit with us—wherever we go. Have I learned to show up, all of me?

Prayer for the Day

Higher Power, help me show up for my life. Help me show up to do my part in Your plan today.

Today's Action

As I go through my day, I'll think about how I'm showing up for my life. I'll be proud of myself for doing my part.

*The present will not long
endure.*

— *Pindar*

At certain moments, our best friend is time.
Time is a gift given to us. Time helps us heal.
We need to know that when things are tough,
these times will pass, and peace will return.
Our Higher Power can be like a parent who
comforts a child when there's a storm outside.
The parent gently reminds the child the sun
will shine again.

Tough times come and go. There will be
times when life is ugly and very painful. We
can't be happy all the time. Remember, our
Higher Power is always there. We must have
faith in this. A saying often heard in the program is, "This too shall pass."

Prayer for the Day

Higher Power, remind me that things will get
better. Even if they get worse for a while, they will
get better. Let this be my prayer in hard times.

Action for the Day

Today, I'll list times in my life when I thought
I couldn't go on. I'll remember the pain, but I'll also
remember how time was my friend.

*The way to love anything
is to realize it might be
lost.*
— *G. K. Chesterton*

Every day we take so much for granted. But we can count certain blessings: a roof over our head, food, clothing, family and friends, freedom, a Higher Power we trust. These things are special. Thinking about them wakes up our happiness. Our recovery program shows us how to be happy. We just have to remember to do what it tells us!

Step Ten helps us wake up our happiness. Each evening, as we think about our day, we can give thanks for the things we love: our recovery, our health, and the special people in our lives. If we spend part of our day thinking about these important areas, we won't lose them.

Prayer for the Day

Higher Power, help me make the most of my blessings today.

Action for the Day

Today, I'll tell five people I love that I'm glad to have them in my life. And I'll tell each of them one reason why.

> *In all the world, there is no*
> *one else exactly like me.*
> — *Virginia Satir*

Let's keep this in mind: each one of us is special in our own way. Often, we're hard on ourselves because we're different.

Our Twelve Step groups pull our differences together. We listen and learn from our differences. We learn to see that each one of us is different—and this is important. Our program and the Steps stay alive for us, because each new person brings a different way of seeing things. Let's celebrate our differences instead of trying to be alike.

Prayer for the Day

Today is a day to celebrate that, in all of the world, there is only one me. Thank-you, Higher Power, and help me see clearly how special I am.

Action for the Day

I'll make a list of what makes me special. I'll share this with a friend or my sponsor and my Higher Power.

When I look at the future,
it's so bright, it burns my
eyes.
— *Oprah Winfrey*

During our illness, it was as if our spirit lived in a deep, dark cave. Our spirit became gloomy, cold, and lonely. Our spirit didn't know how to get out of the cave. We were dying.

Recovery brings us into the sunlight. At first, we can't see a thing—it's too bright! The world stretches around us—it's so big! There are so many ways to go! We don't know what to do.

But then our eyes get used to the light, and we feel the warm rays of the sun. We see we aren't alone anymore. We relax. We know our spirit is in a better place—a place where we can *live!*

Prayer for the Day

Higher Power, help me feel at home in the sunlight of my new life.

Action for the Day

Addiction made my world so small. It made my future so dark. Today, I'll list three new choices I want to make to better my life.

*It's only by forgetting
yourself that you draw
near to God.*
— *Henry David Thoreau*

The biggest danger we face as recovering
people is self-will. Do we try to control others?
Do we always put ourselves before others? Are
we full of self-pity? These are all ways that
bind us to our self-will.

In recovery, we put our lives in the hands
of a loving God. Here, we find a new home.
Our goal is to lose as much of our self-will as
we can. We then put love in place of self-will.
Recovery is truly about love.

Prayer for the Day

Higher Power, I pray and offer my self-will to You.
Self-will is a danger to my sobriety. I pray that I
may be closer to You than to myself.

Action for the Day

I'll list all the areas that self-will gets in my way.
I'll read my list every day next week, and I'll try
to put love in place of self-will.

*Who dares nothing, need
hope for nothing.*
— *Johann Friedrich von
Schiller*

As we grow in recovery, we'll need to change our behaviors, values, and beliefs to stay sane. This takes courage. Courage is doing what is needed in spite of fear.

Courage means facing what we can't change. We can't change the fact that we have hurt people. We can't change the fact that we have an illness. And we can't change the fact that we need help from others.

Courage also means facing those things we can change. We need courage to be honest, to have faith, and to be humble. And we need courage to let people know how important they are.

Prayer for the Day

Courage is more than being tough. Courage means being human. Higher Power, grant me the courage to stay sober and live a spiritual life.

Action for the Day

Today I'll have an attitude of courage. I'll talk in my meeting. I'll offer help where it is needed. I'll have the courage to say no when needed.

*The more one judges the
less one loves.*
> — *Balzac*

At times we need to make judgments about
people's behavior. We stand back and look at
how their lives affect our sobriety. We have to
do this to choose people whose friendships
will be good for us. We have to do this before
we trust someone in business. We should take
a good look at the other person before we fall
in love. But once we decide to trust or love
someone, we have to stop always judging.

When we love someone, we don't stand
back. We move in close. We give them all our
love can offer. We don't just think and judge.
We feel. We are on their side. We look for the
good in them. We don't pick them apart. We
love the whole person.

Prayer for the Day

Higher Power, help me to judge a little and love
a lot. Help me accept the people I love, faults and
all. Help me love them better.

Action for the Day

Today, I'll catch myself when I start to judge
others. I will accept them as they are.

One Day at a Time
        — A.A. program slogan

One Day at a Time reminds us to live in a sane, natural way. It reminds us we can't control the past. It reminds us we can't control the future. We can live only in the present. We have only the moment. We have only today.

Before recovery, our worries about the past and the future put stress in our lives. We need to live in a way that doesn't put us in danger. We need to live in a way that lets us enjoy things. We need to live in a way that lets us stay close to others, ourselves, and our Higher Power.

Prayer for the Day

Higher Power, teach me to really live One Day at a Time.

Action for the Day

Today, I'll keep reminding myself that I have the moment. No more, no less. Am I using my moments the way my Higher Power wants me to?

Nobody ever died of laughter.
— Max Beerbohm

We're not getting sober so we can be more serious. We're getting sober to live. To be free. To laugh and to add more joy to the world. Recovery is about having an even balance between hard work and fun. We work at turning over our will. We do inventories. We drop what we're doing to help a friend in need. We're honest even when it's hard to do. And we learn to have fun. Sobriety needs to be fun.

What are the things you've always wanted to do but were afraid of? Maybe you want to know how to dance. Maybe you want to write poems. Maybe you want to go on a long canoe trip. But you've acted like you don't have the time. Make the time. Have fun! Push yourself to stay fresh in the world! This is the program.

Prayer for the Day

Higher Power, help me to see the funny side of life. Allow me to see humor and fun in my life.

Action for the Day

Today, I'll list the things I like to do for fun. I'll add three fun things I'd like to try over the next few months.

***W**ere entirely ready to have God remove all these defects of character.*

— *Step Six*
from Alcoholics
Anonymous

*Were entirely ready to have
God remove all these
defects of character.*
— *Step Six*

Character defects include being stubborn, feeling self-pity, and wanting to always be in control. We must be ready to give up these defects, or they will hurt us. Being ready is our part of Step Six.

Our Higher Power will remove these defects. We don't need to know how. We just need to be ready to give them up when God asks for them. We don't need to know when. We just have to be ready.

Prayer for the Day
Higher Power, take away my self-pity, fears, anger, and anything else that hurts my recovery. Help me make room for peace.

Action for the Day
Today, I'll get ready to have my character defects removed. I will list them and ask myself, "What do I get from keeping them?"

*God, just for today, please
remove my defects of
character that would keep
me from doing Your will.*
— Cyndy T.

Many of us can't let go of all our character
defects at once. So every day, we can ask our
Higher Power to remove only the ones that
will hurt us today. For example, a character
defect such as laziness won't surface each
day. But on some days, we don't do our Higher
Power's will because of laziness. These are the
times we need to have our laziness removed,
just for the day.

We may not be entirely ready to have our
defects removed forever. But we can give up
a few of them—just for today.

Prayer for the Day

God, just for today, please help me remove my
defects of character that would keep me from doing
Your will.

Action for the Day

I'll say today's prayer three more times during
the day.

*Those whom the gods love
grow young.*
— *Oscar Wilde*

Addiction forced us to grow old fast. Recovery helps us slow down. We regain a youthful spirit. Over time, our excitement for life returns. We are like children on the first day of summer break. We see the world as a place to explore. It won't scare us anymore. We don't run from life. We run into it.

Look around at your meeting; you'll see smiles. Look again and you'll see joy and hope. Look again and you'll see people who are growing younger every day.

Prayer for the Day

Thank you, Higher Power, for allowing me to regain my youthful spirit. Help me grow young.

Action for the Day

Today, I'll watch the children. I will look at their excitement for living and try to be like them.

*We cannot solve life's
problems except by solving
them.*
— *M. Scott Peck*

Before getting into the program, we ran
from problems at all costs. As time went on,
we had more problems. As our problems
grew, we became afraid of life.

The program—the Twelve Steps—teaches
us how to face and solve our problems. We
stop running and stand up to problems. That
way, life's problems scare us less and less over
time.

In fact, life's problems help us better know
our Higher Power and ourselves. We now
know our Higher Power is with us every step
of the way.

Prayer for the Day

I pray for the courage to stand and face life's
problems. I pray for the wisdom to ask my Higher
Power for help.

Action for the Day

Today, I'll list all the problems I now have. I will
talk about them with friends and with my Higher
Power. I will make plans to solve them (sometimes
solving problems means accepting them).

Life is only this place, this
time, and these people
right here and now.
— *Vincent Collins*

Staying in the present can be hard. This busy world pulls our focus from the present. We often wonder if the future will bring good times or bad times.

Life is right before us. Look around. Life is happening—now! The more we live in the moment, the better we feel. Why? Because we can do something about the present. We can't do anything about the future. We have *choices* in the present, and we can do something with our lives. Addiction ran our lives before. Now, with the help of others and our Higher Power, we run our own lives again. This gives us peace of mind.

Prayer for the Day

Higher Power, thank-you for giving back my life. Teach me how to run my life. Have me seek others when I need help. It's okay to ask for help.

Action for the Day

Today, I'll list five things I do well. Then I'll list three things I don't do well. I'll think of people who can help me, and I'll call them.

Fortunate are the people
whose roots are deep.
— *Agnes Meyer*

A tree's roots seek water and minerals. Though the roots can't be easily seen, they are there. The life of the tree depends on them. The stronger a tree's roots, the higher a tree can grow.

We need to set deep roots into the soil of recovery. The soil of recovery is made up of the Twelve Steps, fellowship, and service to others. We'll have to get through storms and high winds in our return to health. In so doing, we'll become beautiful, strong, and spiritual. We'll be able to live with both the gentle breezes and the heavy winds of life.

Prayer for the Day

Higher Power, help me believe in what I can't see. Just as I believe that the roots of a tree are there because I can see the leaves, I believe in a Higher Power because I can see the results.

Action for the Day

I will ask myself, "Which Step do I need to work on the most right now?" I will volunteer to give a meeting on that Step.

Forgiveness is the way to
true health and happiness.
— Gerald Jampolsky

We can't afford to hold grudges. We have all felt hurt by others at times. But when we stay angry at another person, it hurts *us*. It keeps our wounds open. It takes our energy away from our healing.

We can forgive now. We know that living our program of honesty and love makes us safe. We don't have to be afraid. We don't have to be angry. We don't have to let old hurts stand in our way. We let them go. We empty the anger from our hearts to clear the way for love.

Prayer for the Day

Higher Power, help me forgive the people I'm still angry with. Help me see that each of those people taught me something about myself.

Action for the Day

Am I holding on to anger and resentment? If so, I'll make a list today, and I'll talk with my sponsor about ways to let go of them.

*It's not enough to talk to
plants, you also have to
listen.*
— David Bergman

Sometimes, we find ourselves doing all the
talking. When this happens, we need to stop,
think, and listen.

When we do all the talking, we're trying to
control what happens. But when we listen, we
get better results. No one has to be in control.
What a relief!

And we're learning to listen better every
day. It's great—the care, love, and help we
find—just by listening.

Prayer for the Day

Higher Power, help me learn the "give-and-take"
of talking and listening.

Action for the Day

Today, I'll focus on listening, not only to other
people but to my Higher Power's voice.

*Anyone can blame; it takes
a specialist to praise.*
— Konstantin Stanislavski

Are we blamers? We sure were blamers
when we were using alcohol and other drugs.
Then *everything* was someone's fault. Some
of us did our blaming out loud. And some of
us blamed others silently.

It's harder to praise than to blame people.
Faults stand out like street signs, but the good
things about people may be harder to see. We
can see the good in people when we slow
down, watch, and listen.

Prayer for the Day

Higher Power, help me pay attention to people
around me. Help me praise them.

Action for the Day

Today, I'll list three people who mean a lot to me.
I'll write what I like about each of them. I'll talk
to them and tell them what I wrote.

*Never grow a wishbone,
daughter, where your
backbone ought to be.*
— Clementine Pappleford

At meetings, we meet people who have what we want. Our old way is to think these people are better or luckier than us. Our old way is to wish we were like them. But our program tells us how to work for change, not just wish for it. There is a big difference!

There are many ways to work for recovery. We practice the Steps. We attend meetings, and we help out at meetings. We welcome new members. We call our sponsor often. And we sponsor others when we're ready. It takes more than a wishbone. It takes courage and hard work, with the help of our Higher Power.

Prayer for the Day

Higher Power, help me know that wishing is lost energy. I must work at recovery. As I do today's work, guide me.

Today's Action

Today I'll do an extra bit of work on my recovery. I'll call a group member. I'll read. I'll spend extra time in prayer and meditation.

Who is the bravest hero?
He who turns his enemy
into a friend.
— Hebrew Proverb

In recovery we take our worst enemy, addiction, and turn it around. We were ashamed of our addiction. Over time we become proud of our recovery. We were our own worst enemy. Now we're our own best friend. We are brave people.

Being brave is about facing our fears. Often we think brave people don't get afraid, but this isn't true. Brave people learn to stay put, even when their knees are shaking. Many times in recovery, we will want to run when we should stay put. We may even think about using chemicals again. We need to remember our bravery and how we turned our worst enemy into a friend.

Prayer for the Day

Higher Power, teach me when to run and when to stay put. Help me be brave.

Action for the Day

I will claim my bravery today. I'll hold my head up high and be proud of how far I've come. I now have nothing to be ashamed of.

*The lust for power is not
rooted in strength, but in
weakness.*
— *Erich Fromm*

We believed alcohol or other drugs could
help us control our happiness. But now we're
learning to rely on faith for our happiness.
Faith is about leaving things to our Higher
Power's control. Instead of wanting the control ourselves, we trust our Higher Power will
help us handle things that come along.

In recovery, we work at having more faith.
Faith in a Higher Power. Faith in the Steps.
Faith in our groups. Faith that our lives will
get better, if we don't use chemicals and we
work an honest recovery program. Faith
makes life a lot easier.

Prayer for the Day

Higher Power, surround me with Your love. Give
me strength to do hard things. Give me faith to
know that I'm not alone.

Action for the Day

Today, I'll notice how I still want to be in control.
I'll remind myself that it's okay to Let Go and Let
God.

*The reason why worry kills
more people than work is
that more people worry
than work.*
— *Robert Frost*

Worry—it's a lonely activity. It puts distance between us and others. Our program is full of ideas about what to do with worry. In Step Three, we turn our will and lives over to God. This includes our worry.

Our slogans also suggest what to do with worry. One Day at a Time. Live and Let Live. Easy Does It. Let Go and Let God. Their main message is *stop worrying*. Trust the program. Trust your Higher Power. Everything will be okay.

Prayer for the Day
Higher Power, I give You my worries. Teach me how to trust again. I want to trust in You, my program, and myself.

Action for the Day
I'll write the program slogans listed above on a piece of paper, and I'll read them over today. I'll let myself live them today.

*Time is nature's way of
keeping everything from
happening at once.*
                    — Unknown

Time always seems to pass too slowly or too
quickly for us. We want the fun times to last
longer. We want the boring or painful times
to go faster. But time goes at just the right
pace. Any faster, and we wouldn't have
enough time to learn as we go. Any slower,
and we'd lose interest. In our program, we
learn to respect the pace of time. We let go,
and we let time go at its own pace. We call this
patience.

Prayer for the Day

Higher Power, thank-you for patience. Help me
look forward to the future without rushing. Help
me live fully in the here and now. Help me make
today a good one by doing Your will.

Action for the Day

I'll list five ways I can use time to be more
healthy—in body, mind, and spirit. Which of these
five things can I do today?

He who laughs, lasts.
— Mary Pettibone Poole

It feels so good to laugh again! Our disease took away our sense of humor. Recovery gives it back. That's why there's so much laughter at our meetings. By seeing the funny side of things, we ease up.

A person in treatment was talking about the Higher Power he had come to believe in. The counselor asked, "Does your God have a sense of humor?" The group had fun talking about this idea for a while. The next day, the counselor came to work and found a note on her door. It read: "Of course God has a sense of humor. He made you, didn't He?"

Laughter helps us heal.

Prayer for the Day
Higher Power, help me ease up today. Let me see the funny side of things.

Action for the Day
I'll let myself laugh today.

> *A.A. states that resentment
> is the "number one
> offender" among our
> members, that it puts more
> alcoholics in their graves
> than any other thing.*
> — Stools and Bottles

We can get high on anger. That's why it's dangerous. We get a false sense of power from being angry. Our anger turns into resentments. Resentments turn into hate. Hate eats at our spiritual core.

We can get rid of resentments and hate through prayer and helping others. That's why we're to pray for those who have wronged us, so our hearts don't fill with hate. This way, we use our energy in a healthy way. And our serenity will grow as we see that anger no longer has so much power over our actions.

Prayer for the Day

Higher Power, help me stop using anger, resentments, and hate for control over other people and events I don't like.

Action for the Day

I'll list all the people I'm angry at. I'll say a simple prayer for each of them.

*Each day provides its
own gifts.*
— *Ruth D. Freedman*

Life is full of wonderful gifts. Recovery is life's greatest gift to us. If we're not excited about being sober, we need to check on ourselves. Are we keeping something secret? Is there a sadness we need to talk about? Are we stuffing anger? These things eat away at our excitement for life.

Many addicts never get the gift of recovery. Those of us in recovery are special. We've been given a new life. There will be hard times. But the joy of getting a second chance will be stronger. Am I grateful that I've been given recovery?

Prayer for the Day

Higher Power, help me see recovery as a gift. I deserve this gift because I'm human. Help me to always accept this gift.

Action for the Day

At the end of the day, I'll list three gifts that this day has given me.

*Nothing is a waste of time
if you use the experience
wisely.*

— *Rodin*

When we first start our recovery, it hurts a lot to look at our past. We feel sad. It feels like our life was a waste.

But it wasn't a waste. The program promises that if we practice the Steps, we'll not regret the past nor wish to shut the door on it. Hard to believe? Just look at all the happy old-timers in AA. Their lives were just as messed up as ours.

Because of our addiction, we're now learning a *new* way to live. We are getting to know ourselves, our Higher Power, and other people.

Prayer for the Day

Higher Power, thanks for helping me into recovery. Help me learn from my addiction.

Action for the Day

I'll list three important things I've learned about life because of my addiction. I'll talk to my sponsor about them.

*If you tell the truth, you
don't need to remember
anything.*

— *Mark Twain*

One thing that's a lot easier in our life now is this—we can keep our story straight! We are learning that there's one really good way to get along with people: Keep It Simple. Just tell the truth.

It's hard to do at first. We might think, "If people see the real me, what will happen?" We might be afraid of what will happen if we don't lie or make excuses.

But telling the truth works! We find out we never did fool anyone anyway!

Prayer for the Day
Higher Power, make me honest.

Action for the Day
I'll list all the ways honesty will help me in recovery. I'll sign-up to give a meeting on honesty.

Order is heaven's first law.
— Alexander Pope

We need order in our lives. It makes life simpler for us. Life without order would be like driving in a large city without traffic signals. Our lives as addicts were like this. We lived with no plan, no order.

Now that we're sober, we can put some order in our lives. We can get up every morning. We can make our beds and be on time for work. These little things make life so much easier and nicer! We need this order. It allows us to depend on ourselves.

We now look at the Twelve Steps to bring order to our lives. The Steps follow each other as summer follows spring. Do I allow myself to follow the natural order or do I fight it?

Prayer for the Day

Higher Power, You've put order in this world. Please put order in my life. Let me flow within this order instead of being on my own.

Action for the Day

The Twelve Steps have a natural order. Today I'll take time to read each Step and think about the order found in them.

*The future is much like the
present, only longer.*
— Dan Quisenberry

In many ways, we don't know what the future holds. But in terms of recovery, we know the future holds the Twelve Steps. They will be with us for life.

We should never fall into the trap of thinking we "know" the program. We'll *never* know all the truth and love the Steps hold for us. "Knowing the Steps" is a project we'll never finish. As we change, the Steps change.

The Steps are like the seasons. As the seasons come and go, the same field or the same tree becomes a different picture.

Prayer for the Day

Higher Power, I pray for Your help as I work the Steps and continue my recovery. Help me discover new treasures.

Action for the Day

I will ask long-time members of my program how they keep the program fresh and alive.

*The confession of evil
works is the first beginning
of good works.*
— *St. Augustine*

We started recovering the minute we admitted we were powerless over our illness. We crossed over from dishonesty to honesty.

Often, we don't see what power honesty has. Maybe we still aren't sure that being honest is best for us. It is! This is why the authors of the Big Book ask us to be totally honest from the start. Just as denial is what makes addiction work, honesty is what makes recovery work.

Honesty means self-respect. Honesty heals. Honesty lets us look people in the eyes. What comfort we'll feel as we step deeper into our program!

Prayer for the Day
I pray that I'll let go totally. I pray that I'll keep no secrets that could put my sobriety at risk.

Action for the Day
Today, I'll read the first three pages of "How It Works" in the Big Book.

*Words are sacred, we must
use them wisely. . . . They
are a gift of God.*
— *Burton Pretty-On-Top*

We can use words to bring peace to others.
We can use words to tell God and others how
much we care. Or we can use words to hurt
others. We can curse them and scare them
away. We often did this when we used alcohol and other drugs.

In recovery, we learn to use words in a kind,
wise way. We treat words as a gift from God.
We use words to build our relationships.

Do I use words in a kind way? Do I treat
words as a powerful gift from God? Do my
words make the world better or worse for
those who hear me speak?

Prayer for the Day
Higher Power, when I speak words, help me
think about their power. Help me speak to others
in a kind way.

Action for the Day
Today, I'll speak to others with respect. My words
will add a little kindness, honesty, and love to the
world today.

Beauty is a gift of God.
                              — Aristotle

In our addiction, we often went after what was ugly in life. Maybe we hung out in bad places. Maybe we saw people's defects instead of their beauty. Addiction is an ugly, painful disease. The worst part of addiction is how it doesn't let us see beauty in the world.

There is much beauty in each of us. Recovery is beautiful. Our stories are beautiful. The way we help each other is beautiful. The way we become loving family members is beautiful. But sometimes, we may still see the world as ugly. At these times, we need to turn to our program. Maybe we need to help someone by working Step Twelve. Maybe we need to ask to give the Step at our meeting. Maybe we just need to read the Big Book. Whatever we do, one thing is sure—if we turn to our program, we'll see how beautiful the world is.

Prayer for the Day

Higher Power, help me see beauty today. Help me be beautiful today.

Action for the Day

Today I'll let myself feel beautiful. I'll see recovery as beautiful.

*When a man points a
finger at someone else, he
should remember that
three of his fingers are
pointing at himself.*
— *Louis Nizer*

It's so easy to blame others. Others are always making mistakes we can hide behind. That's what blame is—hiding. When we blame others for our mistakes, we're trying to hide our character defects.

It's nobody else's fault that we act the way we do. It's our fault. We're responsible for our actions. And with the help of our Higher Power, we can change. We can turn over our character defects. But first, we have to know them. Then, we give up blaming others for our defects. Over time, we're not afraid to learn about ourselves—even the parts we don't like—because we want to know ourselves better.

Prayer for the Day

I pray for help in facing my character defects.

Action for the Day

I'll think about the past week. I'll list times I've used blame to hide from reality.

*But what is happiness
except the simple harmony
between a man and the life
he leads?*
— *Albert Camus*

Sometimes, we say we're getting our lives together. Together with what? With our selves. The Twelve Steps help us clean up the mess we've made. We're fixing our mistakes. We're looking at ourselves closely—at what we believe, what we feel, what we like to do, who we *are*. We're asking our Higher Power to help us to be our best.

No wonder our lives are coming together! No wonder we feel more peace, harmony, and happiness!

Prayer for the Day
Higher Power, help me remember the best harmony comes when I sing from Your songbook.

Action for the Day
Today, I'll make choices that are in line with who I am.

Hell is not to love anymore.
— George Bernanos

Someone in an AA group said, "From the first day I started this program, I felt like I had died and gone to heaven." This person had walked into a room full of love. In recovery, we are spiritual people because we believe in love. We have faith in love.

Love is respect. Love is truth with kindness. Love is being willing to forgive and help others. Love is thinking about how our Higher Power wants us to act. Love is what we do best. We have turned our will and our life over to love.

Prayer for the Day
I pray that I may love all parts of life. Higher Power, help me seek out love, not material things.

Action for the Day
Today, I'll think about what I love about recovery. I will share this with a couple of friends and my Higher Power.

The closest to perfection a
person ever comes is when
he fills out a job
application form.
— *Stanley J. Randall*

Trying to be perfect gets us in trouble. Trying to be perfect means we're trying to control things. We may be trying to cover up something. Maybe we aren't facing our pain. Maybe we've hurt someone and we need to make amends.

We need to practice being human. Humans aren't perfect. In Steps Six and Seven, we face our human limits and our shortcomings. We then start the lifelong job of letting them go. To accept our human limits leads us to our Higher Power. We see how we need a guide in life. Our Higher Power makes a perfect guide.

Prayer for the Day

Higher Power, help me accept that I can't be perfect. Help me be a good human being.

Action for the Day

Today, I'll list my shortcomings. I'll talk with a friend about them. I'll ask my friend to tell me what my good qualities are.

*I don't believe in the
afterlife, although I am
bringing a change of
underwear.*
— *Woody Allen*

Most of us have many questions about a
Higher Power. Sometimes we have more ques-
tions than answers. No matter how much we
believe about God, there are always questions.
Why do bad things happen if God is good?
Does God punish people?

Is God called Jesus, Buddha, the Great
Spirit? Perhaps we've chosen a name for our
Higher Power, or maybe we haven't. Yet, we
know there is some Power greater than ourselves that's helping us in our recovery.

We know what we need to know about God
for today. We know how to ask for help, and
how to accept help.

Prayer for the Day
Higher Power, help me to know You more clearly.
There's much I'm not sure about. For now, I will
act as if the help I get comes from You.

Today's Action
I'll think of three ways my Higher Power has
done just the right thing for me.

*If you don't know where
you are going, you'll
probably end up
somewhere else.*
— Lawrence J. Peter

The Twelve Steps are our plan for living. We must have a plan. Without one, we waste our energy. We react instead of think. This is what we did as an addict. We lived our lives as out-of-control people. This caused a lot of pain for us and those around us.

Recovery brings us the Twelve Steps, and each Step gives us direction and wisdom. Each Step builds on the progress we made from the Step before it. Sometimes we follow the plan well. Sometimes we think we can do better on our own. Do I believe the Twelve Steps are a good plan of living?

Prayer for the Day

Higher Power, You have shown me a new way of life, a plan for living. Thank you for leading me to the Twelve Steps. Help me follow them.

Action for the Day

Today, I'll take time out to read the Twelve Steps. Then I'll list three reasons why the Steps are a good plan for living.

Humbly asked
Him to remove our
shortcomings.

— *Step Seven*
from Alcoholics
Anonymous

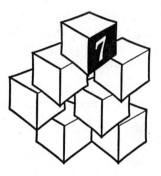

*Humbly asked Him to
remove our shortcomings.*
— *Step Seven*

In Step Six, we got ready to give up our shortcomings. In Step Seven, we ask God to remove them. There is one catch. We *humbly* ask God to remove them.

Being humble means we remember who we are: human beings who need God's help. Being humble means not pretending we're God. We admit we need God's help. Being humble means seeing ourselves as we are. We're a small but very important part of God's plan. We can change much, but only God can change some things about us. This is why we ask. Being humble is not a weakness, but a true strength.

Prayer for the Day
God, please remove my shortcomings.

Action for the Day
Throughout the day, I'll pray to God to remove my shortcomings.

I never think of the future.
It comes soon enough.
— Albert Einstein

None of us know anything for sure about the future. We don't know if we'll be sober tomorrow. But we can be sure of this moment. We get sober by moments. Our sober moments then stretch into hours, days, and years.

Our program tells us to live in the present moment. This is because we can control this moment. We can't control the past or the future. We need to have a sense of control in our life. In our illness, we were out of control. This was because we wouldn't live from moment to moment.

Each moment is filled with as much life as we can handle. Each moment is filled with enough to keep us alive, interested, and growing!

Prayer for the Day
Higher Power, help me find You in each moment.

Action for the Day
Today, I'll stop and focus on the present moment. I will work to see how much control I can have if I stay with the moment at hand.

*We are only as sick as the
secrets we keep.*
— *Anonymous*

It is dangerous for us to keep secrets. Shame builds, and we'll want relief. We may turn to alcohol or other drugs. True relief comes by talking about our secrets, by sharing who we really are with others. Our program helps us live a life based on honesty. Our program helps us battle shame. We don't keep secrets anymore. We start our meetings and share what we tried to keep secret before. "Hi, my name is _____, and I'm an alcoholic." "Hi, my name is _____, and I'm a drug addict." We keep telling our secret, and the shame gets less and less.

Prayer for the Day
Higher Power, I pray to live an honest life.

Action for the Day
I'll list any secrets I've been keeping. I'll talk with my sponsor about them.

I have a dream !
— Martin Luther King, Jr.

During our addiction, maybe we dreamed of joy and laughter with our family—only to find tears and anger. Maybe we dreamed of respect at our job—only to be fired. Our dreams began to feel like burdens. We had lost hope.

With recovery, the hope starts to return. We start to trust ourselves again. We start to trust others again. We start to trust in our Higher Power. Over time, we even dare to dream again. In our dreams, we are loving people. We have something to offer others. We are not scared. This is a sign that hope is returning. We fall in love again with the world, our Higher Power, and ourselves.

Prayer for the Day

Higher Power, thank-you for giving back my future. Thank-you for giving back my dreams.

Action for the Day

Today, I'll tell my dreams to a friend. Do my future dreams include improving myself through the program?

*If at first you don't succeed,
you're running about
average.*

— *Ovid*

Our program speaks of spiritual progress,
not perfection. We can take all the time we
need. Our bottom line is steady progress. We
can ask ourselves, "Am I a little more spiritual
than I was a year ago? A month ago?" If the
answer is yes, we're doing great. If the answer
is no, we should look at why.

Our illness pushes us to be perfect. In
recovery, we learn that we are free to be what
we are—just human. Even the world's fastest
runners are average in most other areas of
their lives. This is okay. Remember, "spiritual
progress, *not* perfection."

Prayer for the Day

Higher Power, I'll not be ashamed of how average
I am. I'll remember I'm average—and that's good.

Action for the Day

I'll list what is average about me. I'll share this
with a friend. Then I'll ask my friend what is special about me.

When fate hands us a lemon,
let's try to make lemonade.
— Dale Carnegie

Our illness is one big lemon, but our recovery is lemonade! None of us signed up to be drunks or druggies, but we all signed up for recovery. That's when the happiness began. Yes, there will be pain, but the joy will far outweigh the pain. The sweet joy of recovery becomes our drink—our lemonade. And, do we drink!

We have new friends. We love ourselves, our Higher Power, our family, and much more. We are creative when we give joy, love, and help to others and to ourselves. If your lemonade isn't sweet enough, add more of your program to it.

Prayer for the Day

Higher Power, it's easy to forget how much You've given me. Thank you for all the joy and love You have given me.

Action for the Day

Today, I'll write down what part of recovery I really enjoy. I will then share this list with my group or a friend.

*Be brave enough to accept
the help of others.*
— Melba Colgrove,
Harold H. Bloomfield,
Peter McWilliams

Often in the past, we acted like we didn't need anyone. It takes courage to let others help us. As we get better, our courage grows. We invite people into our lives. We help others, and we let others help us.

We will learn to let others help us if we work our program. Why? Because we need others to stay sober. When we have a problem, we talk about it in our group. When we need a shoulder to cry on, we call a friend or our sponsor. Over time, our relationships become one of the biggest rewards of recovery.

Prayer for the Day
Higher Power, help me see my need for others as a test—a test to see if I'll be brave enough and wise enough to ask for help when I need it.

Action for the Day
Today, I'll list four times in my life when I needed help but didn't ask for it. I'll tell a friend about how these times would've been different if I had asked for help.

*Pain can't be avoided. It's
as natural as joy.*
— *Unknown*

We got into a lot of trouble trying to avoid pain. We used alcohol and other drugs to avoid pain. We didn't want to accept pain as a fact of life.

We can't avoid pain, but now we have the program. The program teaches us how to talk about our pain. The program teaches how to turn over our pain to our Higher Power.

We don't have to be alone when we face pain. We have friends to go to. Before, when we hurt, we ran to alcohol or other drugs. Now, when we hurt, we run to the comfort of our sponsor and our program friends.

Prayer for the Day

Higher Power, help me accept pain as part of life. Help me remember that You are always there to help me with my pain. I'm not alone.

Action for the Day

Today, I'll list three painful events in my life. I'll talk with a friend about them.

*First say to yourself what
you would be; and then do
what you have to do.*
— *Epictetus*

We often tell ourselves we want to be more peaceful, more in touch with our Higher Power. In other words, we want to become more spiritual. Acting as spiritual people is hard. Too often, we choose the easy way. We make a nasty comment even if we know it'll only make things worse.

We say we have a program for living. Are we living our program? We'll find the answer in our behavior. Sober people act in sober ways. We attend meetings regularly. We study spiritual ideas. We work to bring joy to our lives and the lives of others. Just as we know a good friend by the way he or she behaves, we know a sober person by the way he or she behaves.

Prayer for the Day
Higher Power, help me be a person whose words and actions match up.

Today's Action
Today I'll take an inventory of my actions to see if they are those of a sober person.

*Everybody knows that
when they're happy, then
usually the people around
them are happy.*
— *George Harrison*

Do we think we can't be happy until others are happy? Then nobody is happy. Our unhappy friends won't take our advice. They say, "Why should I do what you say? You are not happy either." And we answer, "I'll be okay when you're happy." We make them responsible for our happiness. What a mess!

We can only make one person happy—ourselves. How? By living as our Higher Power leads us. By working the Steps. By being grateful for the good things in our lives. By loving ourselves and others, *just as we are.*

And maybe when we're happy, our friends will learn from us. They can be happy too. But only our friends can make themselves happy.

Prayer for the Day
Higher Power, as I do my part in Your plan today, help me feel connected to You and to life.

Today's Action
Today I'll enjoy my happiness. I'll look for three ways to share it with others.

*If you would be loved, love
and be lovable.*
— *Benjamin Franklin*

We all want to be loved. And no matter how much we're loved, we always want more.

How can we be lovable? What does this mean? Should we try to be perfect? Should we act cute and helpless? No, being lovable means that we act ourselves. We let others get to know us. When others love us, we enjoy it. We tell them. We let them know that their love isn't wasted on us, that it's important to us.

We are lovable, and we are loved!

Prayer for the Day

Higher Power, help me accept the love of others today. Help me be lovable.

Action for the Day

Today, I'll list all the little things others do that show they care about me.

*Just because everything is
different doesn't mean
anything has changed.*
— *Irene Peter*

Our life changed a lot when we stopped
drinking and using other drugs. But this is
only a start. We need to go further.

Our old attitudes can kill us, even if we
aren't drinking or drugging any more. This
is called a "dry drunk." If we're on a dry
drunk, we've changed the way we act without
changing the way we think.

Our program shows us how to change the
way we think. And we change how we treat
ourselves and others. We learn to live a new
life based on love and care.

Prayer for the Day

Higher Power, help me guard against my old
attitudes. Help me keep changing.

Action for the Day

I'll list four ways I've changed because I'm sober.
I'll list four ways I haven't changed yet.

*A brother may not be a
friend, but a friend will
always be a brother.*
— *Benjamin Franklin*

Many of us come from families that aren't
very healthy for us. Many families have lots
of love but aren't able to show it. Maybe our
parents argued or drank too much. When we
share our recovery with them, they may not
seem happy for us. They may be doing the
best they can, but they don't understand our
new way of life.

We *can* have the love we wanted, but it
might not come from our family. We can
choose healthy friends to be our new "family."
Some friends may seem like the sister or
brother we always wanted. A sponsor can give
us advice we never got from our parents. We
can have a full, healthy "family life" after all.

Prayer for the Day

Higher Power, help me choose good friends who
will help me be the best that I can be.

Action for the Day

The best way to have a friend is to be a friend.
What will I do today to be a friend?

Most of the evils of life arise
from man's being unable to
sit still in a room.
— *Blaise Pascal*

Our program teaches us to slow down. We learn to slow down by taking time out. During these time-outs, we look at our values and see if we're staying true to them.

Because of that, meditation is an important part of our program. It teaches us to slow down. Our Higher Power wants us to have fun and play. But we need to bring our Higher Power along. Remember, our Higher Power loves fun. We can have fun, but not at the expense of others.

Prayer for the Day

I pray for help so I can remember my values. Higher Power, teach me to have fun. Teach me to be true to You at the same time.

Action for the Day

Today, I'll list three times mischief has gotten me in trouble. I'll list three times mischief has been good fun. I'll talk with a friend about the difference between trouble mischief and fun mischief.

*Let there be spaces in your
Togetherness.*
— *Kahlil Gibran*

We all need time alone. Then we can get to
know ourselves better. We can get to know
our Higher Power better too.

When we were using chemicals, we were
afraid of being alone. We didn't want to think
too much. So we got high.

Now we know we're never totally alone. Our
Higher Power is with us. We can relax. We can
rest. We can think, read, meditate. We can be
our own best friend.

Prayer for the Day
Higher Power, help me use my time alone to
know myself better. Help me get to know You too.

Action for the Day
Today, I'll plan to spend two hours alone to get to
know myself better. I could take a long walk, or enjoy a park, or my garden. What will I do, and when?

*We can't all be heroes
because someone has to sit
on the curb and clap as
they go by.*
— *Will Rogers*

Humility is being thankful for the chance to watch the parade. There were days we thought that all that counted were the heroes. But our program has no heroes. It has many fine, spiritual people. . . but no heroes.

When someone is needed to make coffee or pick up after a meeting, we can be willing to do those things. Let's look at doing these little jobs as our way of looking for a good spot on the curb. . . to watch the parade. How good it feels to just sit back and watch the parade! The floats are so colorful, and the bands play so loud!

Prayer for the Day
Higher Power, help me be proud of who I am, instead of always putting myself down because I'm not who I "should" be.

Action for the Day
I will look and help someone today. Service to others is service to my Higher Power.

*Nothing in life is to be
feared. It is only to be
understood.*
— *Marie Curie*

We have many sides, some good, some bad.
Maybe we're afraid to see our faults. But we
don't need to be afraid. After all, we need to
know our dark side before we can change it.
When we see ourselves clearly, we can stop
our dark side from causing trouble.

When we shine light on our fears and
secrets, we'll begin to feel better about ourselves. We'll feel more safe about sharing
our worries. The more honest we are with
ourselves and others, the better and stronger
we become. The goodness and love in us
will blossom. We have a Higher Power and a
program to help us.

Prayer for the Day

Higher Power, help me be brave enough to see
myself clearly. Gently teach me to see who I really
am. Help me know enough to stay sober today.

Action for the Day

Today, I'll look myself in the eyes. I'll spend two
minutes looking into my eyes in a mirror. I'll talk
to my sponsor about what I see.

*It takes twenty years to
become an overnight
success.*
> — *Eddie Cantor*

Successful people make life look easy. But
it's not. Years of hard work, trial and error,
and learning probably went into each
success.

The key is this: We must choose to do what
we really *like*. If we want to be successful,
we'll have to keep working at it. We'll have let-
downs, and we'll get bored at times. But we'll
be happy because we're doing what we want,
what we know is best for us. Real success has
to do with our own happiness.

In our programs, we'll meet many successful people. They've worked hard at recovery,
and they're still learning. And they're happy
to share their success with us.

Prayer for the Day

Higher Power, thank-you for the success the program has already given me.

Action for the Day

I'll list three ways I know I am a success today.
Number one: I'm sober!

*We grow small trying to be
great.*
— *E. Stanley Jones*

We dreamed of being great. Trying to be great is about *control*. We've caused a lot of trouble trying to control things. We've been afraid to just let things happen. We're not very trusting. Many of us have good reasons not to trust. Whatever the reasons, we had put our trust in getting drunk or high. We thought that was one thing we could control. What really happened? We got sick.

Recovery is based on trust. We must learn to trust that it's best for us to give up control. It will seem strange, at first. But letting go and trusting can become a way of life. The Steps, our groups, our sponsor, and our Higher Power—here, we find love and caring. We can trust them.

Prayer for the Day
I pray that day by day, I'll put more trust in my program and in my Higher Power.

Action for the Day
I'll list five reasons why I can trust my Twelve Step program.

*Living so fully, I can't
imagine what any drug
would do for me.*
— Joan Baez

When we were using alcohol and other drugs, our lives kept getting emptier. We tried to keep new things out of our lives. We were scared and tired. We saw feelings as bad. So we got high instead of feeling them.

Now we can live fully every day. We don't want to block our feelings. We aren't afraid of opening up to new things and people.

And the more we open up, the happier we are. Our feelings are free. They bounce around. They don't get stuck. We feel alive. Sure, we feel pain and fear sometimes. But we feel joy, love, and laughter too. And, more and more often, we feel alive.

Prayer for the Day
Higher Power, please help me live fully today. Help me notice my feelings.

Action for the Day
Today, I'll list five things I've enjoyed in the last twenty-four hours.

*There is no human
problem which could not be
solved if people would
simply do as I advise.*
— *Gore Vidal*

Many of us used a "know it all" act to keep people away. We kept everyone around us on edge. They were afraid of our judgments, just as we were secretly afraid of theirs. Why were we so busy with everyone else's life? So we didn't have to look at our own! We were afraid of what was happening to us. But we didn't want to see how sick we were becoming. Now we're not afraid. We don't need to keep people away. We don't need to run their lives. We have our own life to live. And we're enjoying it.

Prayer for the Day

Higher Power, You are the expert, not me. Teach me. I am Your student.

Action for the Day

Today, I'll list the ways I chased away those who cared about me. I'll work on the Steps on these items for the next week.

. . .for, behold, the
kingdom of God is within
you.
— *Luke 17:21*

We want so much to be good. Even when we used alcohol or other drugs, we wanted to believe we were good people. But we often felt we couldn't measure up. We thought we had to live by a set of rules that we could never follow.

Now we're finding the goodness inside us. Goodness isn't something we *do*. Goodness is just being what we already *are*. Our Higher Power speaks to us in many ways, including through our hearts and minds. We don't have to try so hard to be good. We just learn to relax and invite our Higher Power to be a part of our lives.

Prayer for the Day

Higher Power, You have put peace, knowledge, love, and joy in my heart today. Help me to always find these things.

Action for the Day

How's my Higher Power like a loving king or queen? How can I have a kingdom inside me? I'll talk with my sponsor about this today.

*Don't talk unless you can
improve the silence.*
— *Laurence Coughlin*

"Do I talk too much?" Most of us wonder this sometimes. There are some ways to find out.

Ask yourself these questions: "How much do I know about the people in my life?" "What do they think and feel?" "Do I listen to them?" "Do I often feel that I say too much?"

Then ask a few trusted friends these questions: "Do you think I talk too much?" "How well do you think I listen to you?"

Silence helps us listen—to ourselves, to others, and to our Higher Power.

Prayer for the Day

Higher Power, help me enjoy the silent moments in my day.

Action for the Day

Today, I'll think before I speak. What do I really want to say?

*The work of adult life is not
easy.*
— Gail Sheehy

We used to look for an easier, softer way. We
tried to take care of ourselves by staying clear
of hard tasks. The result? We haven't known
what the work of adult life *is*.

The work of adult life is this: to become
spiritually centered. And to do this, we work
at getting rid of our self-will. There will be
many great rewards for doing this. We will
wake up spiritually. We will connect with
those we love. The result? We will receive self-
love to replace self-will. Our work will not be
easy, but it will be rewarding.

Prayer for the Day

Higher Power, help me to give it all to my recovery program. Then help me be open to the rewards
this will bring.

Action for the Day

I will list the hard parts of my program. Then
I'll talk about them with my sponsor, friends, family, and Higher Power.

*If the spirit within us
withers (dies), so too will
all the world we build
around us.*
— *Theodore Roszab*

This is what happened during our illness—our spirits were dying. Our relationships were dying. Our self-esteem was dying. Our love of beauty was dying. This is because addiction is death.

And recovery is life! The Steps breathe life into us. Our groups breathe life into us. We start to heal because we once again feel hope. We're less afraid of what tomorrow may bring. As our hope grows, others feel it too.

We're starting to slowly rebuild our world. We're building our world on the Twelve Steps and their message of hope.

Prayer for the Day

I give myself to life. Higher Power, work with me as I rebuild my world.

Action for the Day

I'll talk with a friend about hope. I'll see my hope as a sign of how close I am to my program.

*I was never less alone than
when by myself.*
— *Edward Gibbon*

To stay in this program, we need to *accept*
that we have an illness. We need to *accept*
that we were out of control. And we need to
accept that we need others and they need us.
At times, we won't want to accept these facts.
We will want to deny we have an illness and
our lives were out of control.

Many of us get into trouble when we don't
accept that we need others. This is why helping others is so important. It teaches us that
we need others, and others need us. By helping others, we learn about the give-and-take of
human relationships. There is no give-and-
take in addiction. There is just take. Now,
finally, we can give too!

Prayer for the Day
I pray to remember that I need other people.

Action for the Day
Today, I'll help out. I will make coffee at the meeting or offer to do the Step next week. I will let a
fellow addict know I'm glad he or she is sober.

*To enjoy freedom we have
to control ourselves.*
— *Virginia Woolf*

Freedom is a funny thing. In a way, it makes life harder. We are free to do what we want, but every choice makes a difference in our lives. Some choices make us happy, and some bring trouble.

We can make good choices. We can control our actions. We can start by having control in little ways: follow the law, pay the rent, make the bed every day. These choices put order in our lives. Eat right, exercise, and get enough sleep. These choices make us strong enough to live each day to the fullest. These kinds of choices set us free.

Prayer for the Day

Higher Power, when I was drinking and drugging, I couldn't enjoy my freedom. I had no control over the little things in my life. Help me stay sober today.

Action for the Day

Today, I'll be grateful for having some control. I will list five ways I am more free because I can control my actions.

*The best leaders are those
who know how to follow.*
— *Anonymous*

Am I a leader or a follower? The fact is, I *am*
responsible for where I end up. If I choose to
be a follower, I'd better follow leaders who
know where they're going. And I had better
know where they're going.

If I choose to be a leader, I'd better know
that I'm responsible for getting myself on the
right path. I also must be honest with my followers, so they can make good choices. I'm
not responsible for my followers' choices, but
I must give them the truth. Being a leader
doesn't always mean I know where I'll end up.
But it can mean that I know I'm on the right
path, following the lead from my Higher
Power—one step at a time.

Prayer for the Day

Higher Power, give me the faith and courage to
choose good leaders to follow. When it is Your will,
help me be a good leader.

Action for the Day

Today I'll list my leaders. They might be a Higher
Power, a sponsor, or a friend. I'll think of why I
choose to follow these leaders.

*They have rights who dare
defend them.*
— *Roger Baldwin*

In recovery, we regain our right to have choices, our right to have honest relationships. Do we claim these rights, or do we let them go by?

Sometimes, standing up for our rights will mean going against the crowd. It will mean turning down that drink when everyone else has one. It will mean telling your honest opinion when it's different from what others think. Being sober will mean, at times, being different. Lots of times, we find being different hard. We want to fit in. This is normal.

But we don't stand alone. We have friends who will stand with us during hard times. We have a Higher Power who will guide and comfort us. We are people with rights. Let's work hard so nothing takes away our rights.

Prayer for the Day

Higher Power, please help me keep and defend my dignity and human rights.

Action for the Day

I'll take time out to list the rights I've gotten back due to my recovery.

*Beauty may be said to be
God's trademark in creation.*
— *Henry Ward Beecher*

Our addiction was like a veil over our heads.
We saw the world as an ugly place. We saw
people as trouble. We thought our drinks and
drugs were beautiful. But even they became
ugly over time. Life became ugly because we
had put distance between our Higher Power
and ourselves.

Now we are blessed because the veil is lifted,
and we are part of the healing process. We
help others step into the beauty of recovery.

Our spirits are again free to seek a relationship with God and others. Through these
relationships, we get our hope back. This hope
helps us focus on the beauty of the world.
Hope is the rain that helps our souls grow.

Prayer for the Day

Higher Power, the world is both beautiful and
ugly. For too long I only saw the ugly. Help me
focus on the beauty.

Action for the Day

Today, I will keep an eye out for the beauty recovery
holds for me. Throughout the day, I'll pray for this.

Less is more.
— *Mies Vander Rohe*

Our program is simple. It has four equal parts: sobriety, fellowship, service, and faith.

Sobriety means we don't use alcohol or other drugs anymore. *Fellowship* means we let people into our lives. We work at having a life that's rich with friends. *Service* means we help when we see a need. It means knowing we have much to offer. *Faith* means we believe in a loving, caring Higher Power. It means using our Higher Power as a guide in life.

Ours is a simple, easy program. Just remember sobriety, fellowship, service, and faith.

Prayer for the Day

I pray that I may keep my program simple. I pray for sobriety, fellowship, service, and faith.

Action for the Day

Throughout the day, I'll remind myself that less is more.

Made a list of all persons we had harmed, and became willing to make amends to them all.

— *Step Eight*
from Alcoholics
Anonymous

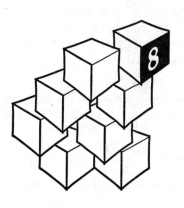

Made a list of all persons
we had harmed . . .
— First half of Step Eight

By the time we get to Step Eight, we're ready to work on our relationships. We start by making a list of all the persons we've harmed. We look at where we have been at fault. We own our behavior.

Now we're healing, and we must help others heal too. Our list must be as complete as we can make it. As our recovery goes on, we'll remember others we have hurt. We add them to our list. By doing this, we heal even more. Remember, this Step is for us. It is to help us stay sober.

Prayer for the Day

Higher Power, help me make a complete list. Help me to keep it open-ended. Allow me and those I've harmed to be healed.

Action for the Day

Even if I've made a list before, I'll make another one today. I will list *all* those I have harmed.

*. . .and became willing to
make amends to them all.*
— Second half of Step Eight

We have made our list of persons we've
harmed. Now we look at how willing we are
to make amends. We might find that we aren't
ready and willing to make amends to everyone. Maybe they have wronged us more than
we have wronged them. Maybe we're afraid
they'll get angry with us. Maybe we're afraid
they'll put us in jail.

We get ready to make amends by listening
and talking to others in our group—and to our
sponsor. We pray for help to be willing to
make amends. Becoming willing does not
just happen. We have to work at it. We need
to be willing to let go of the past.

Prayer for the Day

Higher Power, help me become willing. Help me
see my part. I know "my part" is the only part
I can change.

Action for the Day

I will take time to go over my list. To whom am
I not yet ready to make amends? I will take time
to read the Serenity Prayer.

*Alcoholism isn't a spectator
sport. Eventually the whole
family gets to play.*
— *Joyce Rebeta-Burditt*

One of the biggest lies addicts can tell
themselves is, "I'm not hurting anyone but
myself." This is just another way we don't see
how important we are to others. During our
using, love was a burden. When anyone
showed love for us, we turned away. They
hurt. And we hurt.

In recovery, when ready, we try and help
our families heal. We listen as they speak of
how our illness has hurt them. We comfort
them as they tell their stories. Remember, our
illness hurt them. Remember, our recovery
will help them heal.

Prayer for the Day

Higher Power, help me face the pain my illness
has brought to others. Let me know their pain. Let
it help me stay sober.

Action for the Day

I will list all persons my illness has hurt. I will
say a prayer for them, even if they have harmed me.

*Let him that would move
the world, first move
himself.*

— *Socrates*

Before recovery, most of us were big talkers. The Twelve Steps are for doers, not talkers. In the Steps we find action words: *admitted, humbly asked, made direct amends, continued to take personal inventory.* All of these words speak of action, of doing. Recovery is about action. It's for doers. An action may be very simple. Such as going to a meeting early to set up chairs. Or it could be helping a neighbor. The program teaches that spirituality is action. By being spiritually active, we grow and change.

Prayer for the Day

Higher Power, give me movement. Give me spiritual movement. Help me be a doer, not just a talker. Teach me to work my program.

Today's Action

Today I'll remember that words and action go together.

*You're only human, you're
supposed to make
mistakes.*

— Billy Joel

Listen to the kind voice inside. Listen to the voice that tells you you're good enough. Listen to the voice that tells you it's okay to make mistakes—you'll learn from them. Listen to the voice that tells you to go to your meeting even though it's cold outside and you're tired. Listen, and let this voice become more and more clear. Listen, and welcome it into your heart. Talk with this voice. Ask it questions and seek it out when you need a friend. This voice is your Higher Power. Listen as your Higher Power speaks to you. Listen as your Higher Power tells you what a great person you are.

Prayer for the Day

I pray to the gentle, loving voice that lives in me. Higher Power, You've always been kind to me. You've always loved me. Help me to remember You're always there—inside me.

Action for the Day

I will take time from my busy day to listen and talk with the loving voice that lives inside me.

*Fear of people and
economic insecurity will
leave you...*
— *Alcoholics Anonymous*

We don't have to fear people. They can't wreck our spirit. We don't have to fear money problems. We won't starve to death. Our Higher Power will lead us on a safe path through life.

Our Higher Power wants us to be safe, happy, and wise. Our Higher Power wants us to feel loved. We'll learn to trust our Higher Power. And we'll learn to trust the happiness we find in our new way of life. People may still hurt us, but there will be much more love to carry us through.

Prayer for the Day

Higher Power, I know You protect me and care for me. Help me stop worrying.

Action for the Day

Today, I'll list four fears I have. I will talk with my sponsor about how to turn these over to my Higher Power.

*True enjoyment comes from
activity of the mind and
exercise of the body.*
— *Humboldt*

In recovery, we work at taking better care of ourselves. We care for our mind and our body. Often, during our drinking and drugging, we ignored our mind and body. We probably ate poorly, and we pushed our body to the limit.

But now, we are to recover. . .*totally!* We are to care for our mind and body as we care for our spirit. Our illness is an illness of mind, body, and spirit. So let's care for all three. In recovery, we learn to care for and love *all* of who we are.

Prayer for the Day
Higher Power, help me care for my mind and body as I recover. You love all of me. Help me to respect and care for *all* of me.

Action for the Day
I will write down how much time I've spent caring for my mind and body in the past two weeks. Is it enough?

*Adventure is not outside a
man; it is within.*
— *David Grayson*

Sobriety. It's an exciting adventure. It's a spiritual adventure. We look inward. We find where our Higher Power lives: within us. We then reach outward. We share our joy with others. Not with words and preaching, but by trying to help others. Sobriety is faith turned into action.

Sobriety. It's an adventure in coming to know one's self. At times, we'll have to face our fears. But we'll also find just how much love we have for life.

Sobriety. It's as if we're on a trip. Our Higher Power holds the map. Our job is to listen. And we go in the direction we're told.

Prayer for the Day
I pray to be an adventurer. Higher Power, I pray to follow Your direction.

Action for the Day
I'll ask some friends to tell me about an adventure their Higher Power has taken them on.

If there is no wind, row.
— Latin proverb

At times, staying sober will be easy; at other times, it will be hard. But we must do what is needed to stay sober. Having a hard week? Go to extra meetings. Feeling alone? Call a friend and ask if you can get together. Feel like drinking? Go to a safe place until the urge passes.

We have no choice. We must row when there's no wind. If not, we'll fall back into our addiction.

If we work hard, we'll stay sober. Plus we'll grow as spiritual people. Hard times test us and make us better people. But this will only happen if we keep our Higher Power and our program close to our heart.

Prayer for the Day

Higher Power, help me remember that I grow during hard times. I pray that I'll accept and use what You've given me each day.

Action for the Day

Today, I'll list five things I learned from my program in hard times.

*There are times we must
grab God's hand and walk
forward.*
— *Anonymous*

Sometimes we struggle with being part of the problem, instead of being part of the solution. Inside we know this, but somehow we can't Let Go and Let God.

To let go takes faith that the outcome will be okay. When we have faith, we know our Higher Power believes in us and will guide us. When we have faith, we believe in ourselves. When we let go, we let go of our need to always be right. Letting go first takes place on the inside. Letting go allows us to change how we view what's happening. Often, all we really need is this change of attitude. This is the beauty of faith: it allows us to see the same thing in different ways.

Prayer for the Day

Higher Power, permit me to let go. Let me see that believing in You must also mean believing in myself.

Action for the Day

I will review my life since entering the Twelve Step program. I will work at seeing what good partners my Higher Power and I make.

*The trouble with the rat
race is that even if you win
you're still a rat.*
— *Lily Tomlin*

Alcoholism is a rat race. Drug addiction is a rat race. We were always trying to keep one or two steps ahead of the cat. We were always sneaking around, and everyone was disgusted with us.

Our goal in recovery is to stop acting like a rat and join the human race again. Recovery teaches us sayings like Easy Does It and One Day at a Time. Our sayings remind us to pace ourselves. Our sayings remind us that healing takes time.

We live by human values: honesty, respect for others, fairness, openness, self-respect. We work at just being ourselves. We learn that this is enough. We are enough.

Prayer for the Day
Higher Power, help me accept my humanness. I am part of the human race, not the rat race.

Action for the Day
Just for today, I'll pace myself. I'll list ways I often go too fast for my own good. I'll ask friends how they pace themselves.

*Fairness is what justice
really is.*
*— The late Supreme Court
Justice Potter Stewart*

Some of us get hung up on what's fair. We might feel, because we've worked hard to stay sober, we should be rewarded. We might keep score of what we get and what others get. And we complain if it's "not fair."

Maybe we should be *glad* life isn't fair. Why? Most of us caused a lot of trouble we've never had to pay for. And we've hurt a lot of people who haven't gotten even. Would we really want life to be fair?

Our Higher Power isn't fair either. That is, our Higher Power doesn't keep score. Our Higher Power doesn't try to get even. Our Higher Power is loving and forgiving, no matter what. Our Higher Power has the same love and help for everyone.

Prayer for the Day
Higher Power, give me the wisdom to stop keeping score. Help me want the best for everyone.

Action for the Day
I'll list five times I've been unfair to others. Do I need to make amends?

Once it [a spoken word]
flies out, you can't catch it.
— *Russian proverb*

We've said many mean words. Our words most often hurt the people we love. We can never really take back those words. But we're learning now to speak with care. We know that words have a lot of power.

What do we say when we're angry? When we want something? When we're trying to be kind? Now, think about this: people will remember our words. If we're honest and careful in our speech, people will respect us. But if we say things to force our will, we may be sorry later.

Prayer for the Day

Higher Power, speak through me today.

Action for the Day

Today, I'll ask one question of the person I love the most: "How have my words hurt you in the past?" Then I'll talk with my sponsor about this.

*The best side of a saloon is
the outside.*
— *Anonymous*

We need to stay away from places where we used to drink or use other drugs. Sometimes we need to stay away from our old using friends. But some days it's hard to stay away. We remember the fun times. Or we want a quick fix for our problems. When we feel like this, we know something is wrong. We can call our sponsor and talk about it. And get to a meeting. We need to remember how much better our lives are now. We don't want our old lives back.

Prayer for the Day
Higher Power, help me stay away from trouble. Thanks for keeping me sober today.

Action for the Day
Today, I'll make a list of places that mean trouble for me—places I need to stay away from.

We know what we are, but
know not what we may be.
— Shakespeare

We are addicts. We suffer from an illness.
We go to Twelve Step meetings because we
know who we are. We have a sponsor because
we know who we are. We ask friends for support because we know who we are. We know
why we need our Higher Power to guide us.
Recovery is a spiritual journey. In this journey,
we are followers, not guides. It's a journey that
will change us. We don't know how recovery
will change us, but we know it will. Is my faith
strong enough for my journey? Part of how we
get strong for our journey is by knowing who
we truly are: addicts.

Prayer for the Day

I pray to remember who I am, so I'll learn to
respect the power of my illness.

Today's Action

I'll take time to remember my past, both good
and bad. I'll also take time to think about who I
am now. How far have I come?

The strongest rebellion
may be expressed in quiet,
undramatic behavior.
—Benjamin Spock

In recovery, we each rebel against our disease. Each day we fight for the freedom to stay close to our Higher Power, friends, and family.

It's mainly a quiet battle. It's fought daily. We fight and win by acting in a spiritual way. We fight and win every time we help a friend, go to a meeting, or read about how to improve our lives.

We move slowly but always forward. Rushing will only tire us out. Our battle will go on for life. We are quiet fighters, but we're strong, for we do not fight alone. And we know what waits for us if we lose.

Prayer for the Day

Higher Power, help me stay free. When I want to give up, help me realize this is normal. Help me to keep fighting at these times.

Action for the Day

Today, I'll be a rebel. I will go to an extra meeting, or I'll talk with my sponsor. I'll find a way to help someone without the person knowing.

*Words that do not match
deeds are not important.*
— Ernesto Ché Guevara

What we do can be much more important
than what we say. We tend to talk about
things we *want* to do. We need to also be
people who do the things we talk about. We
are not spiritual people unless our actions are
spiritual.

Many of us used to be "all or nothing"
people. That made us afraid to tackle the big
projects. But now we know we can get things
done, if we take one step at a time. We're not
"all or nothing" people anymore. We're people
who are changing and growing a little every
day. And each day our deeds match our words
a little better.

Prayer for the Day

Higher Power, help me live fully today. Help me
to not just talk about what I want to do. Give me the
gift of patience, so I can be pleased with my progress.

Action for the Day

Today, I'll list the things that I say I'd like to do.
What is one thing I can do today to make each of
them happen? I'll take one step today to match my
life to my dreams.

The Master doesn't talk,
she acts. When her work is
done, the people say,
"Amazing: we did it, all by
ourselves!"

— *Lao-tzu*

Our Higher Power works like the Master. Quietly. In fact, we usually take the credit ourselves!

We're like a child who bakes cookies for the first time. Mother found the recipe, bought the ingredients, and got out the bowl and pans and spoons. She told us what to do, and finished when we got tired. Then she cleaned up after us. We proudly served our cookies, saying, "I made them all by myself!"

In recovery, our Higher Power helps and teaches us every step of the way, just like a loving parent.

Prayer for the Day

Higher Power, *thank-you*—for my life, for my recovery, for love, for hope, and for faith. Thank-you for teaching me how to live in a better way.

Action for the Day

I'll list five ways my Higher Power has acted in my life.

*The future is made of the
same stuff as the present.*
— *Simone Weil*

We found we didn't need magic to recover—
we needed a miracle! Now we are walking
miracles. Part of our miracle is that we see
how important today is. We can't change our
future unless we change today. So we live One
Day at a Time. By living today well, we make
our future better. There is comfort in knowing that the program will be there. Friends
will be there. Hope will be there.

Old-timers say sobriety is easy if we go by
one simple rule: don't drink and go to meetings. Life can get simpler for us. The rules of
life are simple; they don't change much. Staying sober will be easier for us over time.

Prayer for the Day

Higher Power, help me keep my sobriety simple.
Help me accept the rules of life.

Action for the Day

I will list three things that will be there for me
tomorrow and the next day, because I'm working
on them today.

*Heaven and hell is right
now. . .You make it heaven
or you make it hell by your
actions.*
— *George Harrison*

We used chemicals to feel better, but we started feeling worse. We were out of control. Life seemed like hell.

Now we have a program that tells us how to make life better. Some days, it even feels like heaven! But we have to work our program to make our own heaven.

Working the program isn't too hard. And it makes us feel so good. So, why don't we do it all the time? Maybe we're a little afraid of heaven. It's time to learn to love having a better life!

Prayer for the Day

Higher Power, help me work my program each day, so each day has a little bit of heaven in it. Help me get used to having a better life.

Action for the Day

Tonight, I'll think about the moments of kindness, joy, hope, and faith that put a little bit of heaven into my day today.

Beauty is not caused. It is.
— Emily Dickinson

Probably, there have been many times when we thought we weren't beautiful. We thought we were ugly. We thought we were bad people. This is a natural part of addiction. Our program tells us we're good, we're beautiful. Do we believe this? Do we accept this part of our program?

Beauty is an attitude, just as self-hate is an attitude. We need to keep the attitude that we're beautiful. We owe it to ourselves and to those around us. And, yes, it's true that you must love yourself before you can love others. Remember, ours is a selfish program. We have to love and see ourselves as beautiful, before we try to give to others.

Prayer for the Day

Higher Power, help me claim my beauty. Help me to see that, sometimes, I have to be selfish to grow.

Action for the Day

Today, I'll work at falling in love with myself.

It's a rare person who
wants to hear what he
doesn't want to hear.
— *Dick Cavett*

We only want to hear good things. That we're nice people. That our loved ones are healthy. That we did a good job. We don't want to hear that anyone is angry with us, or that we made a mistake. We don't want to hear about an illness or troubles.

But life isn't just happy news. Bad things happen. We can't change that. As we live our recovery program, we learn to handle the hard things without running back to our addiction. We choose the path of life. We need to know all the news, good and bad. Then we can deal with life as it really is.

Prayer for the Day

Higher Power, help me listen—even when I don't want to. Gently help me deal with both the good and bad. All the help I need is mine for the asking.

Action for the Day

I will ask my sponsor and three friends to tell me about my blind spots.

*Where there is no vision, a
people perish.*
— Ralph Waldo Emerson

Working our program teaches us to see things more clearly. We learn to look at who we really are. At first, we're scared to see ourselves. But it turns out okay. We have others to remind us that we're okay, even though we're not perfect.

We also begin to see others more clearly. We see good in people we don't like. And we see faults in people we thought were perfect. But we don't judge people anymore. Nobody is perfect. Just as our program friends accept us as we are, we learn to accept others.

Prayer for the Day

Higher Power, sometimes I don't like what I see. Help me to believe Your way will work for me. Help me have vision.

Action for the Day

I will use my new way of seeing things to avoid trouble today.

*To love oneself is the
beginning of a lifelong
romance.*
— Oscar Wilde

There's a big difference between being self-centered and having self-love. We're self-centered when we think we don't need people. We might think, "I'm more important than others." Being self-centered ends up hurting us. It makes us lonely. It keeps us from our Higher Power. Addiction is about being self-centered.

Recovery and the Twelve Steps are about self-love. If we love ourselves, we'd say, "We're all equal and in need of each other." Self-love includes having good relationships. It includes trusting that we'll do what is best, with the help of our Higher Power. We must believe in ourselves to trust others.

Prayer for the Day
Higher Power, help me love myself as You love me. Help me take good care of myself.

Action for the Day
Today, I'll list three things I like about myself. I'll talk with a friend and share these things. I'll ask my friend what he or she likes about me.

In every real man a child is
hidden that wants to play.
— Friedrich Nietzsche

All of us have a child inside. We may see that child as a friend or as an enemy. Many of us were taught that growing up meant doing away with our inner child. It was as if being a child was bad and being an adult was good. If we try to be only an adult, the child cries, "Let me run free and show you the beauty of the world." If we try to be only a child, we find the adult in us saying, "It's time to grow up."

Let's find a balance. Remember, the adult needs the wonder found in the eyes of the child. Remember, the child needs the loving care of the adult. The child lives where we find our spirit. Our Higher Power is the perfect balance of the two.

Prayer for the Day

Higher Power, help me be both the child and the adult. I need both.

Action for the Day

Today, I'll make time to be a child and to be an adult.

THINK
*— Alcoholics Anonymous
slogan*

Now that we're recovering, our minds are free. We can think. When we are faced with problems or choices, we can do this:

- Ask, "What is the problem?"
- Make a list of what we can do to work on the problem.
- Decide which of the actions on our list might work.
- Pick the action that seems the best so far.
- Ask ourselves, "Can I do it? *Will* I do it?" If not, it's not a good plan.
- Talk to our sponsors if we need help thinking it out.
- Do it.
- Look back on it. Did it work? If not, go back and try something else.

Prayer for the Day

Higher Power, help me to think well. Help me to see things clearly.

Action for the Day

Today, I'll use the points listed above to help me think about a choice I have to make.

Things do not change, we do.
— Henry David Thoreau

There are still as many bars as there were when we were drinking. There are still lots of drugs around. The world hasn't changed. What's changed is that we now live a different way of life. We've learned that, for us, alcohol and other drugs are poison.

For us, there are now two worlds: the world we left behind, and our new world of recovery. In our old world, we'd try to get everyone else to change. We had to be right. In our new world, we look for ways we can change for the better. In our new life, we're willing to change.

Prayer for the Day

I pray that I may be like a mighty river, always changing.

Action for the Day

I will list changes I need to make in my new life.

The saints are the sinners
who kept on going.
— Robert Louis Stevenson

The saints are what our program calls the "winners." We're told to "stick with the winners." Saints are just proven winners. They keep on believing in their Higher Power even when things get hard.

There will be times when we'll want to give up. We may want to stop going to meetings. We may want to get high. We may want to stop working the Steps.

To be winners in this program, we need to follow the example of the saints. This means we live a spiritual life. We need to keep on going. One Day at a Time.

Prayer for the Day

I pray that I'll be a winner in this program. Higher Power, be with me in the easy times and the hard times. Help me keep going.

Action for the Day

I'll list people who are winners in this program. I'll ask one of them how he or she keeps going in tough times.

*This day I choose to spend
in perfect peace.*
— A Course in Miracles

Today, let's be gentle and kind. Let's talk to ourselves with love and respect. Let's be gentle with others too.

Today, let's be clear in how we think, speak, and act. And if we start to get mixed up, let's stop thinking and listen for our Higher Power's voice.

Today, we know that we have just a small job to do. It is to live today with love in our heart. We can't take care of every problem in the world. But we can make our actions today part of the answer instead of part of the problem. Let's Keep It Simple.

Prayer for the Day
Higher Power, help me find Your calmness and peace in my heart today.

Action for the Day
Do I believe that peace starts with me? Today, I'll listen to the simple voice of peace inside of me. And I'll Keep It Simple.

Love is something if you
give away, you end up
having more.
— *Malvina Reynolds*

Service is how we give love away. It's the "self" of self-help. Service is not a duty; it's a gift that's been given to us. We help ourselves by helping others. It's how we make sure the program will be here tomorrow. We "carry the message." It's just one way we see how important we are to others. The world needs us. The world needs our love.

Prayer for the Day
I pray for help in making service a big part of my program. Higher Power, help me to "carry the message."

Action for the Day
Which people could use a kind word and a little love? I will go visit them or give them a call.

*One must never, for
whatever reason, turn his
back on life.*
— *Eleanor Roosevelt*

We're going to have tough times. Maybe we don't get a pay raise. Maybe we get fired. Whatever happens, don't use alcohol or other drugs. Whatever happens, keep working the program. Our program will never turn its back on us. When tough times come, we can always turn to our meetings and sponsors. We're lucky because we don't have to face hard times alone. We have no reason to give up because our program will never give up.

So, pull closer to your program when times get tough. Call a friend and talk about your problems. Take in an extra meeting. All of this keeps us from turning our backs on life.

Prayer for the Day
Higher Power, help me believe that tough times are a chance to get closer to You.

Action for the Day
The program will always be there for me in tough times. Today, I'll make a list of what I'll do to stay sober when tough times come. I'll put the list in my Big Book.

September

*M*ade direct amends to such people wherever possible, except when to do so would injure them or others.

— *Step Nine*
from Alcoholics
Anonymous

*Made direct amends to such
people wherever possible...*
— *First half of Step Nine*

In our illness, we harmed people. In Step Nine, we are to make amends. Making amends is about asking people we have harmed what we need to do to set things right. But making amends is more than saying, "I'm sorry." If you ran a store and someone had stolen five dollars, you wouldn't want them to just say, "I'm sorry." You'd want the person to pay back the money. The same is true with amends.

Many people we've harmed ask only that we don't repeat our mistakes. Respect their wishes. Step Nine has healed many wounds. Step Nine allows us to grow up. Step Nine helps us regain faith in ourselves. Remember, the best amend we make to all is to stay sober.

Prayer for the Day

Higher Power, give me courage. Help me to face the trouble caused by my disease. Make me ready to help others heal from the harm I've caused.

Action for the Day

Today, I'll pray that those I've harmed will heal. I will be responsible for my actions.

*. . .except when to do so
would injure them or others.*
— Second half of Step Nine

We have to be careful when we make amends. We must think about people's well-being. Can we help them heal by being direct with them? Or would this hurt them again?

At times, this means not making *direct* amends. Sometimes, it's better to make some other kind of amend. If you're not sure how to make amends to someone, ask for advice from your sponsor and your group. And pray. Over time, you'll know if making direct amends is the right thing to do. Remember, Step Nine means we're responsible for our actions. In recovery, our actions can be healing. Healing takes place when we love ourselves and others. And love is what heals us.

Prayer for the Day

Higher Power, I've hurt people in the past. Please use me now to help those people heal. Give me good judgment, courage, and good timing.

Action for the Day

I will never be able to make *direct* amends to some people. I will think of other kinds of amends I can make to them. I can pray daily for their healing.

*You will not regret the past
nor wish to shut the door
on it...*
— *Alcoholics Anonymous*

As we work the Steps, we fix our broken life.
Many things in our life have been painful. Our
addiction to alcohol or drugs made it all
worse. But if things hadn't gotten so bad, we
might not have gotten into recovery.

We have changed so much! We have learned
so much! Why? Because we have to learn so
much about life, our Higher Power, and ourselves in order to fix our lives. We can't act
like nothing in the past matters. It does matter, because it brought us to this new life. And
it's better already!

Prayer for the Day

Higher Power, help me face my past and heal the
wounds—my wounds and others' wounds.

Action for the Day

Today, I'll list three things I'm ashamed of. How
can I make amends for them when I work Step
Nine? I will call my sponsor if I need help.

*In my view, we of this
world are pupils in a great
school of life.*

— *Bill W.*

Our addiction has taught us much. It has taught us how far we can get from ourselves, our Higher Power, and those who love us. Hopefully, we've learned we can't go it alone. Do I allow myself to learn from the bad things that happened?

Recovery has much to teach us too. We need to be students of life. We need to be open to learning. Our spirits can grow if we're willing to do three things: First, we listen. Second, we think about what we've learned. Third, we turn what we've learned into action. Listening, combined with thought and action, will help us learn life's best lessons.

Prayer for the Day

Higher Power, You'll test me so I can learn. Help me accept the tasks You give me. And help me learn from them.

Action for the Day

I will view today as a class. I will do three things—listen, think, act.

*I have never seen a greater
monster or miracle than
myself.*

— *Montaigne*

We know we've hurt people. We've heard
our family cry out from the pain we've caused
them. Because of alcohol and other drugs, we
acted like monsters.

But we now live surrounded with love. We
now work hard to make this world better.
Recovery is a miracle. The rebirth of our spirit
is our miracle.

It's no wonder we love life the way we do!
We've been given a second chance. Our joy is
overflowing. Our Higher Power must love us
very much!

Prayer for the Day

Higher Power, help me with the monster that
lives within me. I pray that it will never again be
let out.

Action for the Day

Today, I'll see myself as a miracle. I'll be grateful for my new life.

*Addiction is answering the
spiritual calling inside us by
going to the wrong address.*
— *Chris Ringer*

Where can we go to feel better, to feel
spiritually alive? Not to alcohol or other
drugs. Not to compulsive spending, gambling, or sex. Not to overeating or overwork-
ing. When we turn to these things to feel
better, we're trading one addiction for
another, we're going to the "wrong address."

What is the right address? Our inner needs.
Our Higher Power. Our recovery program. Our
friends. Soon, we become part of a network
of "safe addresses."

Prayer for the Day

Higher Power, keep me on the right path. I don't
want to go to the wrong address anymore.

Action for the Day

Today, I'll make sure I have at least three "right
addresses" in my wallet or purse. I'll list names
and day and evening phone numbers of people
who will love and help me.

*A liar needs a good
memory.*

— *Quintilian*

Many of us wasted a lot of energy trying to keep track of whom we had told what. For example, we'd tell our boss one story and our family another. Then we'd work hard to make sure they never met.

How wonderful to be done with that way of life! We now have a life based on honesty. We can now be ourselves wherever we go.

Our program tells us that to get sober, we must live a life of strict honesty. Honesty is our first rule to get and stay sober. Life is much more simple this way. We can relax and think of the happy details of life.

Prayer for the Day
Higher Power, help me to live honestly. Being honest brings me closer to You. Help me become closer to You.

Action for the Day
Today, I'll read the first three pages of Chapter Five in *Alcoholics Anonymous* (Third Edition). Here, I'll learn why honesty is so important to my recovery.

*I have an intense desire to
return to the womb—
Anybody's!*
                — *Woody Allen*

Some days the world just doesn't seem safe.
Maybe a friend died and you are hurting.
Maybe you argued with a loved one. You just
want someone to take care of you. You want
to feel safe and warm.

Turn to the spiritual part of the program.
Let your Higher Power hold you with warm,
loving care. Pray. Pray to feel the program's
love. If you do this, the love of the program will
find you. Why? Because you've opened your
heart to recovery. To be loved, you have to
open up to love.

Prayer for the Day

I pray for an open heart. I pray that the love of
the program will find me and comfort me. Higher
Power, I need Your love as a child needs the love
of parents.

Action for the Day

Today, I'll list three times the world has felt un-
safe. I'll meditate on how things would have been
different if I had turned to my Higher Power for
comfort.

One of the best ways to persuade others is with your ears—by listening to them.
— *Dean Rusk*

We hate being told what to think. We like to make up our own minds. It helps to talk things out with another person who listens to us. Someone who cares what we think.

We can give this respect to others. We can listen to their point of view. We can try to understand them and care about what they think.

When we do this, others start to care what we think too. We share ideas. The ideas get a little more clear. They change a little. We get a little closer to agreement. We both feel good.

Prayer for the Day

Higher Power, help me know when to listen and when to talk today. Work for me and through me. Thanks.

Action for the Day

Today, I'll look for chances to listen to others when I really want to talk. I'll say, "Tell me more about that." And I'll listen.

*If you want a thing done
"right," you have to do it
yourself.*

— *Anonymous*

We addicts can be very picky. We think there's only one way to do things. It's *our* way, but we call it the *right* way. When we think like this, three things happen. First, we put down other people. Second, we end up doing all the work. Third, everyone feels bad. The other person feels hurt that we don't respect him or her. And we feel angry because we "had" to do all the work.

We need to know that there are many ways to do things. It's okay when others don't do things our way. Their way probably works just fine for them. If they want our advice, they'll ask for it.

Prayer for the Day

Higher Power, help me accept other people and their ways.

Action for the Day

Today, I'll watch how other people do things. Maybe I'll learn a better way to do something.

*This above all: to thine
own self be true.*
— William Shakespeare

What does this saying mean: "To thine own self be true"? Hadn't we thought only of ourselves before recovery? The answer is no. That wasn't the real us. Each of us lost touch with our real self because of our addiction. We lost our goals, our feelings, our values. We chased the high. In this way, we lost our spirit. We became addicts.

With sobriety, we find ourselves again—and it feels great! We stop playing a role and become ourselves—and it's wonderful. We follow our dreams and beliefs, not some addictive wild goose chase. We are again free to be ourselves. Thank you, Higher Power.

Prayer for the Day
Today, I pray to be myself, to know all of me. I can trust myself because my spirit is good.

Action for the Day
Today, I'll pray: "To thine own self be true."

*When angry, count to ten
before you speak; if very
angry, a hundred.*
— *Thomas Jefferson*

Sometimes we just want to yell. Maybe a family member or a friend messed up, and we want to "set them straight." Start counting. Maybe we got chewed out at work and we want "to get even." Start counting.

We can get drunk on anger. We may feel powerful when we "set someone straight." But like an alcohol high, an anger high lasts only a short time and can hurt others. We must control our anger. This is why we count. Cool down. Think out what you need or want to say. Use words that you'll not be ashamed of later. Learning how to respect others when we're angry is a sign of recovery.

Prayer for the Day

Higher Power, teach me to respect others when I'm angry.

Action for the Day

Today, when I feel angry I'll count. I'll work at not controlling others with my anger.

*People seldom improve
when they have no model
but themselves to copy.*
        — Oliver Goldsmith

If we had to get well by ourselves, we'd be in trouble. We've already tried this route. We need to learn a new way to live, not the old way we already know.

That's why we have sponsors in Twelve Step programs. Sponsors are one of the best things about our recovery program. We pick people who are happy and doing well in recovery. Then we copy them. We copy them because sponsors are special people who have what we want. They have sobriety. They have happiness. They have common sense. They have peace and serenity. And they will help us get those things too. We learn a new way to live from them.

Prayer for the Day

Higher Power, help me pick good models. Help me copy what works for them.

Action for the Day

If I don't have a sponsor now, I'll work today on getting one.

*You must look into people,
as well as at them.*
— Lord Chesterfield

When we were using alcohol and other
drugs, we only looked *at* people. We treated
them like objects. Often, we could only see
how they helped us get high, or how they got
in our way.

Now we can see others as people. We look
into them. We learn about their feelings and
thoughts. We care about them. What a wonderful change! We are fully human again. We
can have relationships.

When we look into others, we see life. We
see beauty, courage, hope, and love. We see
bits of ourselves and our Higher Power. What
a miracle life is!

Prayer for the Day

Higher Power, help me be fully human today.
Help me see You in others.

Action for the Day

Today, I'll look into someone. I'll do this by
having a talk with a friend. And I'll *really listen.*

*Often the test of courage is
not to die but to live.*
— *Vittorio Alfieri*

What brave people we are! We have chosen life. Okay, maybe we had a little push, maybe a big push from our family, police, or the pain of our disease. But still, we've chosen recovery. We choose daily to let our Higher Power run our lives. What trust! What faith! What courage!

We work hard at recovery. We do our readings. We go to meetings. We pray and meditate. We look for ways to serve others. Each one of us is building a miracle. We can be proud of this.

Prayer for the Day

I pray that I'll have the courage to love myself. Higher Power, teach me to pat myself on the back when I deserve it.

Action for the Day

I will list three ways I am brave in recovery and share them with my group.

*Here's my Golden Rule: Be
fair with others but then
keep after them until
they're fair with you.*
— *Alan Alda*

Often, in our illness we were ashamed, so
we let people take advantage of us. We acted
as if we had no rights. In recovery, we work
hard to be fair with others. And we deserve
to be treated with fairness too. If people are
mean to us, we talk with them about it. If people cheat us, we ask them to set it right. In
recovery, we live by our human rights.

Prayer for the Day

Higher Power, help me to stand for fairness. Help
me respect myself and others.

Action for the Day

Today, I'll list people who have wronged me. I will
make plans to talk to those with whom I feel will
listen. I will let love, not shame or fear, control my
actions.

*It is better to be wanted too
much than not at all.*
                    — Anonymous

It may seem that so many people want our time and love. Parents say we don't call often enough. Children demand our time. Our partner says we're gone too much. Our sponsor tells us to check in more often.

When we feel off balance by all these people, we need to stop and rest. We need to remember how lonely we were when we were using. No one wanted our time and love then! Now we're important to others again.

You can handle all this by giving people what they need and ask for, within reason— not what *you* think they need, which may be way too much. Maybe you need Al-Anon, too, to learn to love others while still taking care of yourself.

Prayer for the Day

Higher Power, help me put my time and energy to best use today. Help me find the balance I need between work, play, loving others, and self-care.

Action for the Day

When I feel I have to give too much today, I'll stop and ask my Higher Power for guidance.

*We feel that the elimination
of our drinking is but a
beginning.*
— Alcoholics Anonymous

Giving up alcohol or other drugs is just the start. Even if we give up chemicals, can we be happy if we have our old life back in every other way?

We have to do more. We have to see how our illness has changed us. To do this, we turn to the Steps. Our program teaches us to become new persons. We will change. And the changes will make us happy. That's the best part of recovery—change.

Prayer for the Day

Higher Power, make me open to changes that will heal me. Help me see I'm *not* cured just because I've stopped drinking or using other drugs.

Today's Action

Today I'll choose one thing about myself I want to change.

*When we look back, we
realize that the things which
came to us when we put
ourselves in God's hands
were better than anything
we could have planned.*
— *Alcoholics Anonymous*

We can't control the present by looking into the future. We can only look back at the past. The past can teach us how to get more out of the present. But the past is to be learned from, not to be judged.

As we look back, we see the trouble caused by addiction. But we also see recovery. We see how our lives are better. We see our Higher Power's work in our lives. If we honestly look at our past, we learn.

Prayer for the Day

Higher Power, help me learn from the past. With Your help, I'll stop judging my past, just as I wouldn't judge those who have gone before me.

Action for the Day

Today, I'll remember my life before I got sober. Do I still hang on to attitudes or behaviors that might make me start to use alcohol and other drugs again?

*The best way to cheer
yourself up is to try to
cheer somebody else up.*
— *Mark Twain*

Sometimes it does no good to try to "deal" with our feelings. For the moment, we're stuck. We can only see things one way. No matter what anyone says, we're closed up. For the moment. But this puts our sobriety at risk.

How do we stop self-pity? Focus on someone else. When we really want to help someone else be happy, we'll ask our Higher Power's help. Then things start to change, because our good deeds come back to us. Remember, service will always keep us sober.

Prayer for the Day

Higher Power, sometimes I get stuck in my old ways. Help me change my focus at those times. Help me stay sober.

Action for the Day

I will think of a time when I was stuck in bad feelings. How did I get out of that spot?

*Love doesn't make the
world go round. Love is
what makes the ride
worthwhile.*
— *Franklin Jones*

Before recovery, anger, self-pity, and sadness often filled our hearts. The world went
on. We came to hate the ride.

In recovery, love fills our hearts. We begin
to love life. Love is really caring about what
happens to other people. Love is what makes
the ride worth it.

We find much love in our program. People
really matter to us. We really matter to others.
For many of us, we learn how to love in our
meetings. The program teaches love because
the program is love.

Prayer for the Day

I pray that I'll welcome love into my heart and
others into my life. Love brings me closer to my
Higher Power.

Action for the Day

I'll list all the people I love and why they matter
to me.

One Day at a Time.
              — Program slogan

This slogan means we are to take with us *only* the joys and problems of the present day. We don't carry with us the mistakes of days gone by. We have no room for them. We are to work at loving others today. Just today.

It's crazy for us to think we can handle more than one day at a time. During our illness, we lived everywhere but in the here and now. We looked to the future or punished ourselves with our past. One Day at a Time teaches us to go easy. It teaches us to focus on what really means anything to us: the here and now.

Prayer for the Day

Higher Power, help me turn the slogans of my programs into a way of life. Help me to live life moment by moment, One Day at a Time.

Action for the Day

Today, I'll practice living in the present. When I find myself living in the past or in the future, I'll bring myself back to today.

> *. . .he who finds himself*
> *loses his misery.*
> — *Matthew Arnold*

We have lost a lot of misery. In its place inside us, a spirit grows. . .as love is added. Especially self-love. In our illness, we came to hate ourselves. It was really our illness we hated. We couldn't find ourselves. All we saw was what others saw—our illness.

In recovery, we've found ourselves again. We've found we're good people. We've also come to love the world around us. We see we have something to offer this world—ourselves. Why? Because we have found ourselves.

Prayer for the Day
I'm so glad to be alive. At times life hurts, but, in living, I've found You. Thank-you, Higher Power. I pray that we may always be close.

Action for the Day
I will list ten great things I've discovered about myself in recovery.

Martyrs set bad examples.
— David Russell

Sometimes we call people "martyrs." We think of them as victims. They suffer, but sometimes not for a cause. They play "poor me." They want people to notice how much they suffer. They are afraid to really live. These are the people who set bad examples.

True martyrs died for causes they believed in. We remember them because they were so full of energy and spirit.

We can also live a life full of energy and spirit. Recovery helps us live better. Let's go for it!

Prayer for the Day

Higher Power, thanks for giving me energy and for healing my spirit. Help me live fully by putting my life in Your care.

Action for the Day

What kind of example do I set? Does my life reflect joy for life and recovery?

*To speak ill of others is a
dishonest way of praising
ourselves.*

— *Will Durant*

Sometimes we say bad things about others.
When we do this, it makes us look bad too.
Our friends worry what we might say about
them behind their backs. They're afraid to
trust us. We become known as gossips.

The things we say about other people tell
a lot about *us*. We are kind or unkind. We gossip or we don't. This doesn't mean we have
to say everyone is wonderful all the time. As
we work our program to see ourselves better,
we begin to see other people more clearly too.
We see their strong points and their weak
points. But we can know these things without
gossiping about them.

Prayer for the Day
Higher Power, help me see others clearly, and in
their best light. Let me bring out the good in others.

Action for the Day
Today, I'll list the people I'm closest to at work,
school, and home. I'll think of how I talk about
them to others. Am I kind?

*The distance doesn't
matter; only the first step is
difficult.*
— Mme. Marquise du Deffand

During our addiction, we were on a path
leading to death—death of our spirit, mind,
and body. On that path, we tried not to think
about where it would lead. We didn't want to
get there. We just followed the path toward
death, with one drink, pill, snort, or toke at
a time.

Now we've chosen a new path for our lives.
Making that choice was hard. We knew only
the old path. We were afraid to change. But
we did it! That was the hardest part.

We are excited to follow our new path. We
know it leads to good things. We can follow
the map—the Twelve Steps—and enjoy the
trip. It will last as long as we live, and the map
will guide us.

Prayer for the Day
Higher Power, thanks for helping me choose the
path of life.

Action for the Day
Today, I'll study the map for my life by reading
the Twelve Steps.

*Honesty is the first chapter
of the book of wisdom.*
— *Thomas Jefferson*

Honesty is the backbone of our recovery program. Honesty opens us up. It breaks down the walls we had built around our secret world. Those walls made a prison for us. But all of that is now changed. We are free.

Honesty has made us wise. We aren't sneaking drinks anymore. We don't have a stash to protect. People who didn't trust us now depend on our honesty. People who worked hard to avoid us, now seek us out. Self-honesty *is* the greatest gift we can give ourselves.

Prayer for the Day

Higher Power, You are truth. I pray that I may not turn away from the truth. I will not lie. My life depends on honesty.

Action for the Day

For twenty or thirty minutes, I will think about how learning to be honest has changed my life.

*The gift we can offer others
is so simple a thing as
hope.*

— *Daniel Berrigan*

Our actions and beliefs affect others. As we grow and change, we feel better. We view the world with more positive eyes. We must share this with others. We were quick to share our beliefs when we thought life was mixed up and crazy. We need to be just as quick to share our hope.

Each time we tell our story, we must be sure to tell what it's like now. We must tell about our hope for the future. But we must not just *speak* of hope. We must also put our hope into action. We need to become hope—not just for ourselves, but for those who still drink and use, and suffer.

Prayer for the Day

In my hope, I find You. Higher Power, help me to share my hope freely.

Today's Action

If I get stuck today, I'll first reach for the hope found in my recovery. If I see someone who is stuck, I'll share my hope with that person.

*Al didn't smile for forty
years. You've got to admire
a man like that.
— From the TV show,
    "Mary Hartman, Mary
    Hartman"*

Remember how we used to live? We were always trying to cover up some lie or mistake. We were all like Al. Our energy was going into our illness, not into living.

Gratitude is a key word in the program. Gratitude is being thankful for the program. Gratitude is being thankful for getting to know our Higher Power. Remember what it was like to not smile for all those years?

Recovery has given us back our smiles. What a relief! We can relax and enjoy our new life.

Prayer for the Day

I pray that I'll always remember what it was like when I was using. I pray that I'll not take my recovery for granted. I pray for gratitude.

Action for the Day

I will list all the things the program and recovery have given me. I will smile about them today.

*Rarely have we seen a
person fail who has
thoroughly followed our
path.*
— *Alcoholics Anonymous
"The Big Book"*

If we follow the Twelve Steps, we'll leave
failure behind. We may have tried and tried
to be sober, good people, but failed if we were
doing it our own way. Now is the time to stop
listening to ourselves and to start listening to
the pros, those who have gone before us.

When we follow their lead, exciting changes
happen. First, we stay sober. We regain self-
respect. We meet people we respect and become friends. Our families start to trust us
again. And why? Because we gave up doing
it our way and listened. We listened to the
experts.

Prayer for the Day
Higher Power, allow me to become an expert
listener.

Action for the Day
Today, I'll find someone I respect and ask how
they work their program. I'll ask them to share
their wisdom.

*C*ontinued to take
personal inventory and
when we were wrong
promptly admitted it.

— *Step Ten*
from Alcoholics
Anonymous

*Continued to take personal
inventory . . .*
— *First half of Step Ten*

Step Ten tells us to keep looking at who we are. We ask ourselves, "Is what I'm doing okay?" If it is, then we take pride in the way we're acting. If not, we change our behavior. Step Ten keeps us in the right direction.

Throughout time, wise persons have told us to get to know ourselves. Step Ten helps us do this. We become our own best friend. A true friend tells us when we're doing right and when we're messing up. Step Ten is our teacher. Even when we want to pretend we don't know right from wrong, Step Ten reminds us that we do know. Step Ten is our daily reminder that we now have values— *good* values.

Prayer for the Day
Higher Power, Step Ten is a lot of work. Keep me working. Help me form a habit. Let this habit be called "Step Ten."

Action for the Day
Today, I'll continue to take a personal inventory. I will list what is good about me today and what I don't like.

. . .and when we were
wrong promptly admitted it.
— Second half of Step Ten

We are human. We make mistakes. This is
half the fun of being human. Step Ten clearly
tells us what to do when we are wrong: *admit
it.* This keeps us honest. It keeps us from hiding secrets that could cause us to use alcohol
or other drugs again.

Trust is a gift we get from Step Ten. When
we admit our wrongs, people start to trust us
again. We feel good, and people feel good
being around us. Even when they don't like
how we act, they can trust us to run our lives.
No one will ever be perfect. The closest we get
is that we admit it when we're wrong. This
is as good as it gets.

Prayer for the Day

Higher Power, help me admit my wrongs. Help
me earn the trust of others by being honest about
my mistakes.

Action for the Day

I will list any wrongs I've done today. That way,
I'll start tomorrow fresh and without any burdens
from today.

*That which is called
firmness in a king is called
stubbornness in a donkey.*
— *Lord Erskine*

"Rigid" is a fancy word for "stubborn." We addicts can be rigid, stubborn. We act this way because of our fear. When we're afraid, we hang on to what we're used to doing. Our illness had us so scared, we were afraid of new ideas and new people. The only thing that didn't scare us was using alcohol or other drugs.

We also were stubborn when anyone tried to help us. We thought we knew what was best. How silly our stubborn actions made us look! How lonely they kept us!

But our stubborn behavior can teach us about our fears. We need to be aware of our stubbornness. Then we'll be able to find out what we're afraid of—and do something about it.

Prayer for the Day

Higher Power, help me know when I'm stubborn.

Action for the Day

Today, I'll work at accepting my stubbornness. I will use it to learn about what I am afraid of today.

*Your three best doctors are
faith, time, and patience.
— From a fortune cookie*

Only a short time ago, we were very sick. Getting sober made us so much better. At first, when we stopped drinking and using other drugs, we thought we were fixed. Then we began to see that we were not all that well.

No doctor can fix us. To get well, we need to keep on living by the Twelve Steps and the slogans of our program. We need to keep on trusting that our Higher Power will heal us. One Day at a Time, day after day, we get stronger and happier. And it never has to stop. Each day, we know ourselves a little better.

Prayer for the Day

Higher Power, You are my best doctor. Help me remember that.

Action for the Day

Today, I'll do what the "doctor" suggests. I will talk with my sponsor about Step Ten today.

*It is often easier to fight for
one's principles than to live
up to them.*
— *Adlai Stevenson*

It is easy to talk about our values. But when
the clerk at the store gives us extra change by
mistake, those values get put to the test. It
feels good to read about spirituality in a com-
fortable chair at home. But when we get stuck
in a traffic jam, it's hard to live by our values.

That's why practicing our program *daily*
helps. Practice prepares us for the tough
times. Maybe we'll only feel like drinking or
using other drugs once a year. Maybe we'll
only get the wrong amount of change once
a year. But if we live our values daily, we'll be
ready when the hard times come. Remember:
"It's not enough to talk the talk. You have to
walk the walk."

Prayer for the Day

Higher Power, help me live this program each
day. Help me "walk the walk."

Action for the Day

Today, I'll do a Step Ten. Taking an inventory tells
me if I'm living up to my values.

*If you do not tell the truth
about yourself, you cannot
tell it about other people.*
— *Virginia Woolf*

Working the Twelve Steps helps us learn the truth. As we struggle with Step Four, we learn the truth about ourselves. We learn even more about ourselves by doing Steps Eight and Ten. When we admit the truth about ourselves, things come into focus. Big changes happen.

As a result, we can see other people more clearly. We see bad sides in people we thought were perfect. We see good sides in people we hated. We start to know that everyone has to work hard to find what's right for them. No one knows all the answers.

In short, we begin to trust others who also are looking for the truth.

Prayer for the Day

Higher Power, help me clearly see myself and others.

Action for the Day

Today, I'll think about how doing Step Ten keeps me clear about what's going on in my life.

*We never thought we could
get old.*
— *Bob Dylan*

Here we are, no longer children. Yet we're
not quite grown up either. At least, we don't
always *feel* grown up. Our program helps us
accept the stages of our life. We're children
in our hearts all our life. And the child in our
heart is getting happier. In some ways, we feel
younger every day.

We're also starting to feel older and wiser.
It feels good. We're not so afraid of the world,
because we're learning better ways to live in
it. We can learn by having friends who teach
us to stay young at heart.

Prayer for the Day

Higher Power, help me be the best I can be, at
the age I am today.

Action for the Day

Today, I'll call an older friend and ask him or her
this question: "What's the most important thing
you've learned about life since you were my age?"

Just Say No.
— *Nancy Reagan*

We addicts were great at saying *no*. Our spouse asked us to help around the house, but we said *no* and went drinking. Friends tried to care, but we said, "No, mind your own business!" Our parents or our kids begged us to stop drinking, but we said *no*.

We were also good at saying *yes*. We always said *yes* when asked if we wanted to have a drink or get high. Addiction really mixed us up. When we said *no*, we should've said *yes*. And when we said *yes*, we should've said *no*.

In recovery, we do things better. We say *yes* when others ask for help. We say *yes* when someone wants to give us love. We say *no* to alcohol and other drugs. We finally answer *yes* or *no* the right way—the right way and at the right time for *us*.

Prayer for the Day

Higher Power, help me to always say *yes* to You, even when I'm tired or angry.

Action for the Day

In today's inventory, I'll ask myself if there are any ways I'm still saying *no* to my program and Higher Power.

*A man should never be
ashamed to own he has
been in the wrong...*
— *Jonathan Swift*

In the past, we felt a mistake was a crisis. We thought we had to be perfect. Our old way was to try to hide our mistakes. We were ashamed. We thought making mistakes meant we were bad.

Mistakes are normal. We can learn from our mistakes. They can teach us. They can guide us. The Tenth Step directs us to *promptly* admit when we're wrong. Then, over time, we start to see mistakes as normal life events. As we face and correct our mistakes, shame is washed away. We feel lighter. We know it is normal to make mistakes.

Prayer for the Day

Higher Power, help me see that mistakes are normal life events. Help me promptly admit when I'm wrong.

Action for the Day

Today, I'll talk to my sponsor about the mistakes I've made the past week. I'll not act ashamed of my mistakes.

*The foolish and the dead
never change their opinions.*
— *James Russell Lowell*

We need to stay fresh in our program. We need to be open to new ideas. We need change. The ways we work the Steps should change for us as the years go by. And as we grow, more of the fog of our denial clears away. Then we see the world and our program in different ways.

We need to allow this to happen. At times, it's scary to give up old ways and old opinions, but this is what allows new growth. Every day, we wake up to a new world. Being alive means change. Being alive in our program will also mean change. Opinions and ideas are like a strong tree: the base is strong, but the leaves change with the seasons.

Prayer for the Day

Higher Power, help me stay fresh and alive. Help me stay open to new ideas and attitudes. Help me to not become rigid.

Action for the Day

Today, I'll ask two friends to tell me how I may be rigid. I will listen to what they say.

*May you live all the days of
your life.*
— *Jonathan Swift*

The truth is, life is hard. Accepting this fact
will make life easier. Remember how well it
worked in Step One? Once we admitted and
accepted that we were powerless over alcohol
and other drugs, we were given the power
to recover. It works the same with life's
problems.

We can spend a lot of energy trying to avoid
life's hardships. But our program teaches us
to use this same energy to solve our
problems. Problems are chances to better
ourselves and become more spiritual. We
have a choice: we can either use our energy
to avoid problems, or we can face them. When
we stop wasting energy, we start to feel more
sure of ourselves.

Prayer for the Day
Higher Power, life is to be lived, both the easy and
the hard parts. Help me face and learn from it all.

Action for the Day
I'll work at not complaining about how hard life
is. I'll take the same energy and use it to solve
problems I may face.

*Trust only movement. Life
happens at the level of
events, not words.*
                    — *Alfred Adler*

Being sober is an event. Being sober also means movement. We *go* to meetings. We *find* and *meet* with a sponsor. We *talk* with friends. If we don't act in these ways we're not sober.

Our actions also tell us if we're leading a spiritual life. What do you *do* when you see someone in need? Spirituality means helping. It's not just kind words.

In Steps Four and Ten, we check out our actions, not our words. Our actions will tell us if we're on the recovery path.

Prayer for the Day

Higher Power, help me to not hide in my words. I pray for the strength to take the right action. Help me walk a sober path.

Action for the Day

Today as I work Step Ten, I'll focus only on my actions. How have I *acted* sober today?

*Self-pity is one of the most
dangerous forms of self-
centeredness. It fogs our
vision.*

— *Kathy S.*

Sometimes, we get stuck in our own way of
seeing things. We may feel as if everything
that happens, happens to us or for us. If it
rains, we may think about our ruined picnic
and not about the dry fields that need rain.
We need to focus on the big picture. This
keeps us from becoming self-centered. If it
rains, we'll gather indoors and be glad for the
farmers. When we do our part, things go well.
When we don't, we feel it. Everyone else feels
it too. Self-pity keeps us from doing our part.

Prayer for the Day

Higher Power, help me see myself as part of a big
picture. My job is just to do my part.

Action for the Day

Today I'll think about how I fit in with my Higher
Power, my family, the place I work, my community.
Do I do my part?

A baby is God's opinion
that the world should go on.
— *Carl Sandburg*

Recovery is also God's opinion that the world should go on. But when we used alcohol and other drugs, there were days when even the sight of a newborn baby couldn't bring hope into our hearts. We were spiritually dead. We didn't care if the world went on. We didn't care about anything but getting high.

Through recovery, our souls come alive. The beauty of a fall day can reach our hearts. We can see the miracle found in a baby's eyes. We can see the beauty of the world. We can feel how much we're loved by our Higher Power and by others. This is how we know we're alive. Hope fills our minds and love fills our hearts.

Prayer for the Day

Higher Power, now that I again believe the world should go on, have me work to improve it. Have me be a person who makes the world more beautiful.

Action for the Day

Today I'll notice the children and babies around me. I'll notice how alive they are. I'll try to be as alive as they are.

Not to decide is to decide.
— *Harvey Cox*

We are winners, because every day we decide to stay sober. Every day we decide to listen to our Higher Power. We win by making active choices. We've stopped acting as if we have no choice. Our old way was to pretend that everything happened to us by accident. Not true. We pretended we had no power. Also not true. We lost our power over alcohol and other drugs, but we still had the power to ask for help. Each time we used chemicals was a decision, just as to stay sober each day is a decision.

It feels great to know we aren't victims. We like ourselves again. We smile as we hear the strength in our voices. We walk as proud and sober men and women who know how to make decisions.

Prayer for the Day

Higher Power, thanks for giving me choices. I will not run from them. Help me make good choices. Help me decide every day to listen to You.

Action for the Day

Not for one minute will I pretend I am a victim. I'll face my choices squarely and decide.

*To err is human, but when
the eraser wears out ahead
of the pencil, you're
overdoing it.*
— *Josh Jenkins*

It's okay to make mistakes. But we shouldn't live a life of excuses. We shouldn't slide over our mistakes; we should learn from them.

Excuses keep us apart from ourselves and others. People don't trust us if we won't admit and accept our mistakes. Relying on excuses dooms us to repeat the same mistakes.

In recovery, we admit and accept our behavior. We do this by continuing to take an inventory of our lives. We do this so we can learn from our mistakes. "Owning" our mistakes helps us grow.

Prayer for the Day
Higher Power, help me own my mistakes. Thank-you for Step Ten and the growth it holds for me.

Action for the Day
Today, I'll list my five favorite excuses. I'll think of the last time I used each of these. What was I trying to avoid?

Every child is an artist.
The problem is to remain
an artist once you grow up.
— Pablo Picasso

We each have colorful ideas waiting to be shared. We're alive inside. But do we let this side of us show? Our disease stole much of our childlike openness. Many of us were taught that growing up meant denying the child within us. Many of us grew up in homes where it wasn't safe to act alive and creative. Whatever the reason, it's time to claim the child, the artist, in each of us. Each of our programs is different, and each has its artistic touch. When we tell our stories, we share our lives. And our lives are unique and alive. The more alive we become, the more color we bring to others and ourselves. Let's not be afraid to add color to our lives.

Prayer for the Day

Higher Power, help me claim the child inside of me. Joy is a choice. Help me choose it.

Action for the Day

Today, I'll work at not hiding myself from others. I'll be alive, and I'll greet everyone I meet with the openness of a child.

> *If God wanted us to be*
> *brave, why did he give us*
> *legs?*
> — *Marvin Kitman*

Many of our problems are caused by taking an unwise stand. We end up being stubborn. We need the courage to know when to take a stand, and the wisdom to know when not to. Our program has taught us not to stand up to our drinking and other drug use, but to walk away from it. It beats us every time we stay around it. When we walk away we can get help. By walking away, we stay sober and we win.

Step Ten can help us learn when and where not to take a stand. If we take a stand just to be stubborn, we must surrender and admit this is wrong. That way, we learn how to take a stand for good reasons.

Prayer for the Day

I pray that I may stand for recovery. I pray that I'll surrender when I'm just being stubborn.

Action for the Day

Today, I'll list how I get stubborn. I'll list what Steps help me to surrender to my Higher Power and to the program.

> *A wise man changes his mind, a fool never will.*
> — *Seventeenth century proverb*

We addicts used to be stubborn. Once we got an idea in our heads, we wouldn't change it. We didn't listen to other ideas. We almost seemed to say, "Don't tell me the facts. I've already made up my mind."

But lately, some new ideas are making sense to us. We are starting to change our minds. Maybe we *are* good people, after all. Maybe we *do* deserve to be happy. Maybe other people *can* help us. Maybe our Higher Power *does* know best.

We're not acting like fools any longer. We're learning to change our old ideas.

Prayer for the Day

Higher Power, when I hear a better idea, help me change my mind.

Action for the Day

When I hear or read a new idea today, I'll really think about it. If it fits, I'll try it.

*We lie loudest when we lie
to ourselves.*
— *Eric Hoffer*

When we're not honest with others, we're not being honest with ourselves. In recovery, we're taught how to heal our hearts. We admit we're wrong, and we do it quickly. We let our spirit speak out. We listen to our spirit. We let our spirit have the loudest voice. This way, lies lose power over us. We find a way to be true to our spirit.

Prayer for the Day

Higher Power, You have a soft, quiet voice inside of me. Help me, through meditation, to hear You better. Yours is the voice I want to follow.

Action for the Day

I'll listen to my Higher Power. I'll list any lies I've been telling myself and others lately. Then I'll find someone I trust and tell that person what I've lied about.

Even a stopped clock is
right twice a day.
— *Anonymous*

Nobody's always wrong. Nobody's all bad. And that includes us.

Sometimes, we really get down on ourselves. When we do Step Four, we sometimes see only our faults. When we make our Step Ten checkup, we see only our mistakes. We can't afford to do this. We need to see our strengths too. But even our faults have a good side. Are you stubborn? Good—be stubborn about staying sober. If you're stubborn, you know how to hang on to feelings. So, hang on to the good feelings instead of the bad ones.

Each of us is good and wise. What's good about us got twisted by our disease. But now we can get the kinks out. We are sober, and we have a program to help us.

Prayer for the Day

Higher Power, help me to see the good in myself and others.

Action for the Day

I'll take another look at my faults today. How can I use them in good ways?

*Life is what happens to us
while we're making other
plans.*
— *Thomas LaMance*

What happened to our years of drinking
and using other drugs? They seemed to pass
so quickly with so little to show for them. We
had plans, but we didn't get where we wanted
to go. There was always "tomorrow."

What a difference today! Now we work a
program that helps us really live each day.
We're not losing time out of our lives anymore. Now every day is full of life: sights,
sounds, people, feelings—those things we
used to miss out on. We have the help of a
Higher Power who makes every day important.

Prayer for the Day

Higher Power, help me do Your will for me today.
I place this day in Your care.

Action for the Day

Be on the lookout today for signs of life!

*It's not dying for faith that's
so hard, it's living up to it.*
— *William Makepeace
Thackeray*

We may ask, "Do I have to do an Eighth or Ninth Step?" "Do I really need a sponsor?" "Hmm...can I get by without going to so many meetings?" Having faith means putting our questions aside. So...what *do* we do? We work the program. We accept that those who've gone before us were right. We accept the idea that we need others. Faith is knowing that others love and care for us. Faith is also about action. The main way we know that we have faith is by looking at our behavior. Ask yourself this: "Are my actions those of a person with faith?"

Prayer for the Day

Higher Power, help me remove the questions that get in my way. Help me act like a person with faith.

Action for the Day

I'll list four parts of my program that I have faith in, such as, "I believe honesty is important to my sobriety."

*Sin has many tools, but
a lie is the handle that
fits them all.*
— *Oliver Wendell Holmes*

Lying, above anything else, brings us close to getting crazy again. Lying is what addicts do. In our addiction, our whole life was a lie.

Lying creates danger because it creates secrets. Secrets keep us from others. To stay sober, we need to stay close to people. We can't make it on our own.

Lying creates danger because it creates shame. A lie, like a drink, may make us feel good for the moment. But in the long run, it creates shame.

Do we still lie to deal with the world? Why? There is no such thing as a small lie. Lies are like drinks—one leads to another.

Prayer for the Day

Higher Power, help me to live today free of lies.

Action for the Day

For the next twenty-four hours, I will tell no lies. If I do, I'll go back and do Step Ten. I will remember that lies can lead to relapse.

*Love thy neighbor as
thyself, but choose your
neighbor.*
— *Louise Beal*

In our program, we learn a lot about loving ourselves. Then we start to see how this helps us love our neighbors. We learn to love ourselves honestly, seeing our strengths and our weaknesses. We learn to see others honestly. We learn how much to trust ourselves, and when to get extra help. We learn how much to trust others too. We learn to love ourselves with a love that's honest and challenging. We learn to love others this way too. We learn to care about others without losing our common sense. We learn to protect our spirit from harm.

Prayer for the Day

Higher Power, help me see others clearly. Help me love them. But help me choose carefully who I trust.

Action for the Day

Today, I'll list three people I trust the most, and I'll write down why.

*Nobody can give you
freedom.*

— *Malcolm X*

We were not free. We were prisoners of our
illness. What our illness wanted, we gave it—
our dignity, our self-respect, even our families. Our prison walls were made of denial,
false pride, and self-will run riot. Now we
know that brick walls don't have to stop us.
We don't have to bang our heads on them.

Slowly, we're learning about freedom. We're
learning that freedom comes from within. It
comes when we think clearly and make our
own choices. It comes when we follow a better
way of life. It comes when we take care of ourselves. It comes when we take responsibility.
The key to freedom is in loving our Higher
Power. Do you choose freedom?

Prayer for the Day

Higher Power, show me how to walk away from
a wall or go around it. But teach me to stop and
think when I get to a wall. Maybe it's there for my
safety.

Today's Action

Today I'll think about all the freedom I have given
myself by living a sober way of life.

An excuse is worse and
more terrible than a lie.
— Alexander Pope

Excuses. They're lies. We use excuses to hide from ourselves. Maybe we don't want to be honest about our anger. So we say someone else made us angry. Maybe we don't want to admit how mean we can be. So we pretend we have no part in what happens.

Excuses keep us from ourselves. They keep us from our Higher Power. A lot of our program is about looking at ourselves. Steps Four, Five, and Ten tell us to be honest about our excuses. We can be honest because we are good people. We are loved.

Prayer for the Day

Today, I'll say the Serenity Prayer: God grant me the serenity to accept the things I cannot change, the courage to change the things I can, and the wisdom to know the difference.

Action for the Day

I'll list my five most often used excuses. Then, I'll share them with my friends, family, and sponsor. I'll ask them to tell me when I make excuses.

*I wish you the courage to
be warm when the world
would prefer you to be cool.*
— *Robert A. Ward*

Our program and the Steps have warmed us—warmed us from the inside out. Just as a bonfire warms those who stand around it, the Steps take away the chill we have felt for so long.

At times, we'll be tempted to move away from the Steps. At times, we'll get tired of looking at our behavior and attitudes. We are, by nature, controlling people. We'll want to "prove our point" about something when our program tells us to let it go. We need to stay close to the Steps and the warmth they hold. Remember the chill of our disease.

Prayer for the Day
I need to remember that the Steps and the fellowship of the program keep me sober, not me alone.

Action for the Day
Today, I'll think about what the Steps have done for me. I will think of how they have kept me warm.

*Each morning puts a man
on trial and each evening
passes judgement.*
— Ray L. Smith

In many ways, the Tenth Step is very natural. We continue to take a personal inventory. And when we're wrong, we promptly admit it.

At the end of each day we ask ourselves, "How did my day go?" As we think about our day, we bring order to our life. The Tenth Step teaches us about order. It also teaches us how to correct mistakes. We do this by admitting our wrongs. This way, we have no backlog of guilt. It's good to start each day fresh, free from guilt. Admitting our wrongs is a loving thing to do. It's another way the program teaches us to love ourselves.

Prayer for the Day
Today, I'll face many choices. Higher Power, be with me as I choose. When the day is done, remind me to think about how I lived today. This will help me learn.

Action for the Day
Tonight, I'll list three choices I made today. Would I make the same choices again?

*The universe is full of
magical things waiting for
our wits to grow sharper.*
— *Eden Phillpots*

How nice to have the fog lifted! Sobriety lets
our wits grow sharper. We can go after our
dreams and ideas. We can listen to music and
sing. We are part of the magic of the universe.
At times we may not feel very magical, but
we are. Our spirits hold much magic. Sobriety
is magic. We work at making the world a
better place. In doing so, we get magical
powers. Powers that heal and comfort others.
Powers to understand things that before we
could not. Powers that let us see the world as
we've never seen it. Enjoy the magic and use
your powers wisely!

Prayer for the Day

Higher Power, let Your magic enter and fill my
heart.

Action for the Day

I'll list four magical powers I have from being
sober.

*A man who has committed
a mistake and doesn't
correct it is committing
another mistake.*
— *Confucius*

Step Ten tells us that when we are wrong, we must "promptly" admit it. We aren't used to admitting our mistakes. We defend ourselves or blame others. This is called *denial*.

Denial is bad for two reasons. First, it keeps us from learning from our mistakes, so we keep making them. Second, we don't listen to others, so we close off ourselves and become lonely.

What a relief it is to admit our wrongs! We don't have to keep trying to do things the hard way. We can learn new ways to think and act that will work better for us. We can let other people be our teachers.

Prayer for the Day

Higher Power, help me out of denial, so I can see the changes I need to make.

Action for the Day

Today, if I disagree with someone, I'll promptly admit it when I'm wrong. If I'm right, I'll be gentle. I don't have to prove anything.

Sought through prayer and meditation to improve our conscious contact with God as we understood Him, praying only for knowledge of His will for us and the power to carry that out.

— *Step Eleven*
from Alcoholics
Anonymous

*Sought through prayer and
meditation to improve our
conscious contact with God*
as we understood Him . . .
— *First half of Step Eleven*

Through Step Eleven, we develop a lasting,
loving relationship with our Higher Power.
Conscious contact means knowing and sens-
ing God in our lives throughout the day.

God is not just an idea. We talk with our
Higher Power through prayer. As we meditate,
we sense God's love for us, and we get answers to our questions. When we pray and
meditate, we become aware that God is always with us. Simply put, we're not alone
anymore. Our Higher Power becomes our best
friend. Our Higher Power is there for advice,
support, celebration, comfort.

Prayer for the Day

Dear Higher Power, I pray that our relationship
grows stronger every day. I accept the friendship
You offer me.

Action for the Day

Today, I'll seek out God through prayer and
meditation.

*. . . praying only for
knowledge of His will for
us and the power to carry
that out.*
— Second half of Step Eleven

Step Eleven teaches us how to pray. We pray
for God's will to replace ours. Our will got us
in trouble. God's will guides us to simple
serenity. We pray for power to live a spiritual
life. This is important, for it takes much
strength and courage to live a spiritual life.

The sober path is not always easy. It takes
self-discipline. We have to say no to our self-
will. We follow God's will for us. The rewards
are great. We get sobriety. We get serenity. We
get friendship. We regain our family. We get
a deep, loving relationship with a Higher Power who wants peace and joy for us and for the
world.

Prayer for the Day

Dear Higher Power, I pray the words of Step
Eleven. I pray to know Your will for me. And I pray
that I have the power to carry out Your will.

Action for the Day

I will examine my life. I will look to see how my
will gets in the way of God's will.

Words are the voice of the heart.

— *Confucius*

What does my heart have to say today? Am I happy? Or am I troubled? We will find this out if we slow down and listen to our words. We can also hear our spirit in the tone of our words.

We are to meditate. Meditation is about slowing down so we can hear what our spirit is trying to tell us. Meditation is listening. Our spirit is but a quiet whisper inside us. To hear it we must quiet ourselves.

Slowing down allows us to find our center. As we find our center we find our spirit and our Higher Power. Do I take the time needed to slow myself down? Do I take the time to listen—to listen to my heart?

Prayer for the Day

Higher Power, teach me to slow down. Teach me to listen. Teach me to hear Your whispers as well as Your yells.

Action for the Day

Today, I will take a half hour to slow down and listen. I will find a place to relax and listen to my heart and my words.

*Each day comes bearing its
gifts. Untie the ribbons.*
— Ruth Ann Schabacker

How full life can be! We can untie the ribbon on this gift by keeping our spirits open. Open to life. Open to how much our Higher Power loves us.

Who knows what gifts the day may bring? Maybe it brings a solution to a problem. Maybe it brings the smile of a child. Maybe we'll find a new friend. Whatever gifts the day brings, we must be able to receive them. How do we do this? We keep our spirit open and lively through prayer and meditation. Then we'll be awake to see the beauty and the wonders life holds for us.

Prayer for the Day
Higher Power, remind me to pray to You often. Remind me to stop and listen to You. Remind me that You love me very much.

Action for the Day
At the end of the day, I'll take time to list the gifts I've been given today. This will be first on my list: I am sober.

*Acceptance and faith are
capable of producing 100
percent sobriety.*
— *Grapevine*

Acceptance and faith are the most important parts of our recovery. If we boil down
Steps One and Two, we'll find acceptance and
faith. *Acceptance* means we see the world as
it is, not as we want it to be. We start to see
ourselves as humans, not as gods. We are
good, and we are bad. We need to fit in the
world, not run it.

Acceptance also guides us toward faith
Faith is believing. We start to believe that
someone or something will take care of us.
Faith is about giving up control of outcomes.
We learn to say to our Higher Power, "Thy will
be done."

Prayer for the Day

Higher Power, help me accept my illness. Give
me the faith to know that You and I, together, will
keep me sober.

Action for the Day

Throughout the day, I'll think of the Eleventh
Step. I'll pray to my Higher Power, "Thy will be
done, not mine."

*That suit is best that best
suits me.*
— *John Clark*

How much time do we spend trying to
"fit in"? Many of us used to care so much
what other people thought about us—our
clothes, our ideas, our work. Did we drink
the right brand, drive the right car, listen to
the right music?

In our program, we still have to watch out
for fads and peer pressure. We have to ask
ourselves if we're really in touch with our
Higher Power. Are we searching for a sponsor
who has inner peace and direction? Or do we
look for people who are like our old using
friends? As we learn to find our own way of
following our Higher Power, we need to be
okay with being different.

Prayer for the Day

Higher Power, help me be the best me I can be
today.

Action for the Day

Today, I'll work to be me—honestly me—to everyone I meet.

*Telling the truth is a pretty
hard thing.*
— *Thomas Wolfe*

Often, we get scared to tell the truth. We
wonder, "What will happen? Will I get in trouble? Will someone be mad at me?" These
things could happen. But good things could
happen too.

Sometimes we want to lie. We don't want
anyone mad at us or unhappy with us. We
want people off our back. So we lie. And it
comes back to haunt us. We must believe that
the best will happen in the long run if we tell
the truth.

Our program tells us that we can stay sober if
we're honest. Telling the truth takes faith. We
must have faith in the program. We must be
honest. Our sobriety and our life depend on it.

Prayer for the Day
Higher Power, help me remember that I'm doing
things Your way when I tell the truth.

Action for the Day
I will think about what I say today. I will be as
honest as I can be.

*Any man may make a
mistake; none but a fool
will persist in it.*

— *Cicero*

The way we face life's challenges is what gives meaning to our lives. If we run from our mistakes, they follow us. If we stand up and work with them, we learn.

Facing our mistakes teaches us wisdom and courage. Our self-respect grows. Spiritual growth means asking, "How would my Higher Power want me to deal with this mistake?" Then we listen for the answer and do what is needed.

The better we get at facing our mistakes, the better we become at learning from them. Native American culture teaches us that all mistakes in life are gifts. The gift is that we are given a chance to learn.

Prayer for the Day

Higher Power, help me face the mistakes of life and find the lessons that lie within them.

Action for the Day

When I make a mistake, I'll stop and ask, "What does my Higher Power want me to learn from this?"

*He who can take advice is
sometimes superior to he
who can give it.*
— *Karl von Knebel*

In recovery, we learn that we don't know everything. We had stopped listening. Most of us had been asked by family, friends, doctors, and employers to stop drinking and using other drugs. But, we didn't listen. If we had listened, we would've been in this program long ago. Addiction did something to how we listen. We heard only what we wanted to hear. Do I still hear only what I want?

In recovery, we learn to listen. We listen to our groups. We listen to our sponsor. We listen as we read. The better we listen, the better our recovery.

Prayer for the Day
Higher Power, open my ears and eyes to this new way of life. Allow me to hear Your wisdom in the Twelve Steps. Allow me to be someone who takes advice, not just gives it.

Action for the Day
Today I'll try to listen. Today I'll seek the advice of others. I'll ask my sponsor how I may better my program.

*Even if you're on the right
track, you'll get run over if
you just sit there.*
— *Will Rogers*

The greatest adventure ever is recovery.
And action is what's important in recovery.
That's because the Twelve Steps are full of
action. The whole world has now opened up
to us. At times, this will scare us. But we
aren't alone. Our Higher Power is there to help
us. All we have to ask ourselves is, "Would
this action keep me in touch with my Higher
Power?" If the answer is yes, then we take
action. If the answer is no, then we don't.

In recovery, we'll be busy. We admit our
wrongs. We take inventories. We seek
answers. We ask for help. We are to get as
much as we can out of life. We can't sit and
watch; we have to get out and live life.

Prayer for the Day
Higher Power, You gave me a second chance at
life. Help me use it and not let my fear stop me.

Action for the Day
Today, I'll list five things I want to do but am
afraid to try. I'll talk to someone I trust about how
I can do these things.

*Have the courage to live;
anyone can die.*
— *Robert Cody*

Living means facing all of life. Life is joy *and* sorrow. We used to be people who wanted the joy without the sorrow. But we can learn from hard times, maybe more than we do in easy times. Often, getting through hard times helps us grow. When things get tough, maybe we want to turn and run. Then, a gentle voice from within us says, "I am with you. You have friends who will help." If we listen, we'll hear our Higher Power. This is what is meant by "conscious contact" in Step Eleven. As this conscious contact grows, our courage grows. And we find the strength to face hard times.

Prayer for the Day

I pray for the strength and courage to live. I pray that I'll never have to face hard times alone again.

Action for the Day

I'll list two examples of "conscious contact" in my life.

It may be those who do
most, dream most.
— *Stephen Leacock*

Daydreaming gives us hope. It makes our world bigger. Daydreaming can be part of doing Step Eleven. As we meditate, we daydream. Through our daydreaming, we get to know ourselves, our spirit, and our Higher Power. What special work can we do? Our dreams can tell us.

There is time to work and time to dream. Daydreaming helps us find the work our Higher Power wants us to do.

Prayer for the Day

Higher Power, please speak to me through my daydreams.

Action for the Day

I'll set aside time to daydream. I will look into a candle flame, at a picture, or out a window, and let my mind wander.

*Write down the advice of
him who loves you, though
you like it not at present.*
— *Anonymous*

We addicts often learn things the hard way.
In the past, we found it very hard to take advice from anyone. It's still hard to take advice,
but it's getting easier every day. We know now
that we can't handle everything in life by ourselves. We've come to believe there is help for
us. And we're learning to ask for help and
advice.

Sometimes we don't like the advice we get.
We don't have to use it. But if it comes from
people who love and understand us, we can
try to listen. Write it down. Think about it. It
may make sense another day.

Prayer for the Day

Higher Power, please work through people who
love me. I need Your advice. Help me listen to it.

Action for the Day

I will make notes to myself, writing down things
that seem important. I will read them once in a
while.

*Make it a point to do
something every day that
you don't want to do.*
— *Mark Twain*

Self-discipline is a key part of living a sober life. We need it to get to our meetings regularly. We need it to understand the Steps. We need it to work the Steps.

And we get much in return. With self-discipline, we learn to trust ourselves. We learn to do what is most loving and caring for ourselves. What a great relief! One of the worst parts of our illness was that we couldn't count on ourselves. We didn't know what we'd do next. Self-discipline heals this part of our illness.

Prayer for the Day

Higher Power, You have given me much. It's only right that I give You part of my day. I will pray and meditate on Your wonders.

Action for the Day

I will list areas of my program where I lack self-discipline. I will share the list with my group and sponsor, and I'll let them know in a month how I'm doing.

*The best way to know God
is to love many things.*
— *Vincent Van Gogh*

Now that we're in recovery, we're learning to love people. We're learning to love nature. We're learning to love new ideas about life. The result? We love the way we feel now that we're taking care of ourselves.

Is our Higher Power really so close? Can we really find our Higher Power just by loving many things? Yes! When we love, we wake up that part of us that is part of all creation— our spirit. We really come to life when we love!

Prayer for the Day
Higher Power, remind me that You are near when I love someone or something. The energy of love comes from You.

Action for the Day
I will list three things I love that help me know my Higher Power is near me.

*Pray for powers equal to
your tasks.*
> — *Phillips Brooks*

Our task is to stay sober and to help others who still suffer from addiction. We will need patience and understanding. We will need much love. Most of all, we'll need to work a strong program.

Pray that you come to know the Steps well. Pray that you'll want to help others—always. Pray for courage and wisdom. Pray for these things, and you'll have a strong program. In the program, we learn that prayer works. We see prayer change our lives and the lives of those around us. We came to know the power of prayer.

Prayer for the Day

Higher Power, I pray for knowledge of Your will for me and the power to carry it out.

Action for the Day

Today, I'll admit my needs by praying for help from my Higher Power.

Mishaps are like knives,
that either serve us or cut
us, as we grasp them by
the blade or the handle.
— Herman Melville

We have hung on in hard times. We made it through our addiction. Some of us have lived through abuse. We've felt like our hearts were broken. But we've proven *we are survivors.* Now we're learning that we can *heal.*

Being in recovery doesn't mean things will be easy. But we have a Higher Power to help us. We have friends who listen to us, care for us, and help us through the pain. Because of our recovery program, we're able to keep hope and love in our lives—One Day at a Time.

Prayer for the Day

Higher Power, help me through the hard times. Help me trust in Your love and care.

Action for the Day

Today I'll plan ahead with my sponsor. What will I do now so that I'll have strong support when hard times come?

Life is short: live it up.
— Nikita Khrushchev

We won't stay sober for long unless it's more fun than using chemicals. The truth is, using chemicals wasn't fun anymore. It was work. We just *told* ourselves it was still fun.

So live it up! Try new things. Meet new friends. Try new foods. Taking risks and having adventures are a basic human need. So go for it. Sobriety is fun. Living a spiritual life is fun. Get out there and live!

Prayer for the Day

Higher Power, teach me to play. Teach me to have fun. Teach me to live!

Action for the Day

Today is for fun. I'll try something new. I'll see how many people I can get to smile. And I'll celebrate the fact that I'm sober.

*What we don't live, we
cannot teach others.*
— Day By Day

Remember—we don't carry the message to others until we get to Step Twelve. We must first learn to live in a sober way. Sobriety takes time. We have to stop using alcohol and other drugs, but this is only the start.

Just as it takes time to build a home, it takes time to build a new way of life. We talk with friends and sponsors about the Steps. We try using them in our lives. Then we talk about how the Steps work for us. We talk about where we get stuck with the Steps.

All this takes time. We aren't in a hurry. We have a lifetime ahead of us. Remember— the better we live our program, the better we help others.

Prayer for the Day
Higher Power, You'll let me know when I'm to carry the message. Until then, be with me as I build a new way of life—a sober way of life, a spiritual way of life.

Action for the Day
I'll take time to think over where I'm at with my program. I'll talk about it with a friend.

*A man is too apt to forget
that in this world he
cannot have everything. A
choice is all that is left him.*
— H. Mathews

Sobriety is about choice. Each day we choose to stay sober, we teach ourselves how to make better choices.

Life is about choice. To be spiritual people, we must make spiritual choices. Honesty is a spiritual choice. And working the Steps is a spiritual choice.

Our life is the sum total of our choices. We owe it to ourselves to choose wisely. We can do that now, thanks to the program.

Prayer for the Day
Higher Power, help me choose a spiritual way of life. Help me to see choice as my way to a better relationship with You.

Action for the Day
Today, I'll be aware of the many choices I make. At the end of the day, I'll think about all the choices I've made. Am I proud of my choices?

*To love others, we must
first learn to love ourselves.*
— Anonymous

Sometimes we think our life would be fine
if that dream person showed up. But loving
someone isn't easy. Our bad habits cause
problems. We have to change. Sometimes we
aren't ready to have one special person. We
need to have a group of people—our recovery
group—to love and help us get healthy. We
must learn to trust, to be honest, to give help,
and to love others. The truth is, no one person can make our life wonderful—except us.
We hold happiness inside of us. It's in our
spirit. Look no further.

Prayer for the Day
Higher Power, help me love myself.

Action for the Day
I'll list five ways I will love myself today.

*We are healed of a
suffering only by
experiencing it in full.*
— Marcel Proust

We must never forget our past. We need to remember the power that our illness has over us. Why? So we can remember how our recovery began. So we can remember we're not cured. So we can tell our stories.

We must remember how we acted. Why? So we can look at our behaviors every day. So we don't act and think like addicts. Most of us had poor relationships with friends, family, and ourselves. We need to remember how lonely we felt. That way, we'll make our recovery grow stronger One Day at a Time.

Prayer for the Day

Higher Power, help me always remember how my illness almost destroyed me. Help me face the pain of these memories.

Action for the Day

I will talk about my past life with those who support my recovery. I will tell them what it is that I must remember about my past.

*Let me listen to me and not
to them.*
— *Gertrude Stein*

Often, we try to please everyone around us.
But this may not make us happy, and so we
get angry. We feel taken advantage of.

We may be kind to others, but first we must
love ourselves. How? By learning to listen to
ourselves. To our dreams. To our Higher Power.
By doing this we'll be more happy. And those
around us will probably be more happy too.

As our AA medallions say, "To Thine Own
Self Be True."

Prayer for the Day
I pray that I'll listen to that gentle, loving voice
inside me. Higher Power, help me make my "conscious contact" with You better.

Action for the Day
I will write four reasons why I need to be true
to myself.

Freedom is not enough.
— Lyndon B. Johnson

We are free of alcohol and other drugs. We've been given a second or third chance. For that, we thank our Higher Power. We've started a new life. But to keep this life, we need to change. We need new friends. We need to let a Higher Power guide our hearts, minds, and bodies. We need to learn new values and how to stand up for them. We need to learn how to give and to receive.

Freedom from dependence is not enough. We also want to be happy, and to do something with our lives. So each day we keep learning, we keep growing. Each day without alcohol or other drugs is a gift, a gift from God.

Prayer for the Day

Higher Power, You set me free. Now teach me to stay free. Guide me, for keeping my freedom is a big task.

Action for the Day

I will meditate on my freedom. I will take time to list all the ways I am now free.

Love is the reward of love.
— Johann von Schiller

When we used alcohol and other drugs, we shared as little as possible. There was little love in our hearts. We had become selfish. This caused us to be lonely.

Then something happened to change all of that. Remember the first time you walked into a meeting? You were met by people who shared. Maybe they shared a smile, their story, or just a cup of coffee with you. The sharing that goes on in a Twelve Step program is great. We learn that the more we give, the more we get. We get well by giving to others. Helping others is a great way to hold on to sobriety. Love is the reward of love.

Prayer for the Day

I pray that I will be there when others need me. I pray that service will become a big part of my program.

Action for the Day

Today, I'll think of friends who could use my help. I'll talk to them and offer to be there for them.

*It's gonna be a long hard
drag, but we'll make it.*
— *Janis Joplin*

Some people start each day with a groan. They act like staying sober is no fun at all. They may have turned over their illness to their Higher Power. But they haven't yet turned over their *will* and their *life*. They don't see that a loving Higher Power can change them into happy people.

Maybe they don't want to change. They just want to feel better. After all, that's one reason we all took drugs—to feel better without changing. The program asks us to be willing to *change*. That's how we become happier people.

Prayer for the Day

Higher Power, help me listen to Your voice. Teach me that following Your directions will make me happy.

Action for the Day

Today, I'll list three things in my life that I haven't yet turned over to my Higher Power. Why are these things so important to me? What can I do to turn them over?

*Life is not lost by dying; life
is lost minute by minute, day
by day, in all the thousand,
small, uncaring ways.*
— *Stephen V. Bénet*

Our Twelve Step program promises us a
new way of life. But most of us won't just wake
up one day with a new attitude. We only gain
this new way of life if we get involved.

The Twelve Steps are *tools* to build a new
life. The more we use a tool, the easier it is
to use. The same goes for the Twelve Steps.
We need to depend on the Twelve Steps, just
as carpenters depend on their tools. If we only
wait for the new way of life, it'll never come.
The quicker we get involved, the quicker we'll
get fixed.

Prayer for the Day

Higher Power, help me get involved. Help me
build a new way of life.

Action for the Day

Today, I'll look for ways to use the Twelve Steps.
If I have a problem, I'll first stop and think of how
the Twelve Steps can help me solve it.

The purpose of freedom is
to create it for others.
— Bernard Malamud

Sobriety is freedom. With this freedom, we have a responsibility to help other addicts who still suffer. The program tells us this in Step Twelve. We do this by telling our stories and offering hope.

We must be ready to care, to give of ourselves. This is what spirituality is about. When we help others, we prepare the road for those who enter the program after us.

Tradition Five of the Twelve Traditions says, "Each group has but one primary purpose— to carry its message to the alcoholic who still suffers." It means we get better by helping others.

Prayer for the Day
Higher Power, help me create more freedom. Bring me to where I'm needed. Help me carry the message well.

Action for the Day
Today, I'll think of ways I can help the addict who still suffers. Then I'll choose one way I can be of help. I'll talk with my sponsor about it, and I'll follow through with my plan.

*One is happy as the result
of one's own efforts.*
— George Sand

Happiness is not an accident. It comes from following the spiritual voice found in each of us. This isn't always easy. Sometimes, the voice tells us to do things we're afraid of. For example, if we're lonely and the voice tells us to call someone on our phone list, we may make excuses to not do it. Again, the voice may say, "Just make the call. It will be okay." If we follow the voice, we'll find happiness.

The spiritual voice inside us speaks of care and love. It will never tell us to hurt others or ourselves. It is our Higher Power's voice. It's what Step Eleven calls "conscious contact." If we follow this guiding voice, it will lead us to happiness.

Prayer for the Day

I pray that I'll come to know my Higher Power by listening to the spiritual voice in me.

Action for the Day

Today, I'll meditate and listen to my Higher Power's gentle voice within.

*There is no fear in love, but
perfect love casts out fear.*
— 1 John 4:18

Love is allowing another person to be part
of you. When we love someone, we feel the
person inside of us. Spiritual love is letting
our Higher Power become part of us. We feel
our Higher Power inside of us. This is what
is meant by "conscious contact" in Step
Eleven.

When we were drinking and drugging, we
kept others on the outside. Inside we felt bad,
and we didn't want anyone to be close to us.

We are now asked to open ourselves up to
love and its healing power. Part of the joy of
love comes from letting another person know
us. You may even wonder, "Will people stick
around if they really know me?" Love will
answer, "Yes."

Prayer for the Day
Higher Power, let me trust Your love. Then I can
give up my fear.

Action for the Day
Today I'll invite my Higher Power into my heart.
I will practice conscious contact.

*H*aving had a spiritual
awakening as the result
of these steps, we tried to
carry this message to alcoholics,
and to practice these principles
in all our affairs.

— *Step Twelve*
from Alcoholics
Anonymous

*Having had a spiritual
awakening as the result of
these steps...*
— First part of Step Twelve

We are awake! Our spirits are alive. We
are part of the world. Our addiction no
longer clouds our vision. How? Step Twelve
answers this.

The beauty of Step Twelve is that if we feel
our spirits starting to go dead, we know how
to awaken them. It's simple. Turn to the Steps.
After all, working the Steps has awakened our
spirits. The hope and serenity we feel are gifts
given to us through the Steps of our program.
And the more we turn to the Steps for help,
the more life we'll feel. The Steps are what
feed and heal our souls.

Prayer for the Day

Higher Power, thank you for the Steps. If I start
to believe it is I who keeps me sober, remind me
of my life before the Twelve Steps.

Action for the Day

Today, I'll read the Twelve Steps. I'll think of how
each Step helped awaken my spirit.

DECEMBER 2

*. . .we tried to carry this
message to alcoholics. . .*
— *Second part of Step Twelve*

In this part of Step Twelve, we carry the message of hope. But it's not up to us if anyone accepts the message or not. This keeps us from playing God. We just gently deliver the message. We don't force the program down people's throats.

In general, Step Twelve tells us, "Be helpful to those we can help." When a neighbor is sick, mow her lawn. When a friend is in the hospital, visit him. Step Twelve reminds us that we make a difference. We have hope to give the world. And hope is what we stand for to the addict who still suffers. Hope is what we stand for to the addict's family. How beautiful to stand for hope! Remember when our lives stood for despair? What a change!

Prayer for the Day
Higher Power, help me shine brightly as a symbol of Your hope.

Action for the Day
Today, I'll help someone in need. It may be an alcoholic or other drug addict, or just someone in need. I'll help make the world a better place.

*. . .and to practice these
principles in all our affairs.*
— *Third part of Step Twelve*

This is a statement about us. We are now people with values. These values reflect our spiritual growth. We know how to help others. We know how to admit our wrongs. We know how to look at ourselves and change our defects. We know how to live an honest life. Step Twelve tells us, "Go use these tools for better living. Go be all you can be. Enjoy life and live a life you can be proud of."

Step Twelve also tells us about how to have loving relationships. By the time we complete Step Twelve, we make or regain many relationships. The most important one is with our Higher Power. As we grow in the program, we realize all our relationships are spiritual gifts.

Prayer for the Day

Higher Power, I now have one face instead of many masks. Help me be a person who will stand before You with pride, not shame.

Action for the Day

Today, I'll talk with a friend and talk about my new values. I will talk about how much my life has changed.

*The measure of a man's
real character is what he
would do if he knew he
would never be found out.*
— *Thomas Macaulay*

We must live our new life all the time. This is what the Twelfth Step means by practicing "these principles in all our affairs." We try to be honest all the time. We don't cheat, and we tell the truth when asked a question. We learn that even if we can get away with something, we can't get away from ourselves.

This makes our lives so much easier. Our relationships, and our spirituality, get built on solid ground. We also come to trust in ourselves. We depend on ourselves to do the right thing—and we do. How nice it is to count on ourselves!

Prayer for the Day
Higher Power, make me strong enough to practice the Twelve Steps in all my affairs.

Action for the Day
Have I done anything that's bothering me? If so, I'll set a time to talk about it with my sponsor. The two of us can figure out how to solve it.

*Each day, somewhere in
the world, recovery begins
when one alcoholic talks
with another alcoholic,
sharing experience,
strength, and hope.*
— *Alcoholics Anonymous*

All over the world, recovering men and women use the same Twelve Steps to live their lives. Our fellowship keeps on growing. The bigger it gets, the faster it grows. Why? Because the program brings our spirits back to life. All over the world, many of us were dying, and now we're full of life and love. We are bringing our world back to life. As we share our experience, strength, and hope, we help others join us in coming back to life.

Prayer for the Day

Higher Power, help me stay sober today. Guide me and all others who are doing Your will today.

Action for the Day

Today, I'll think of three things I can do to help spread the message of A.A. and N.A.

*The strongest of all
warriors are these two—
Time and Patience.*
                    — Leo Tolstoy

One of the first things we learn about in recovery is time. Before, we may have tried to control time by pushing it along. We tried to hurry everything and everybody. We wanted our "quick fix." But the program tells us to slow down. Easy Does It.

We probably couldn't picture ourselves staying sober for the rest of our life. So we were told to just work at staying sober today. We learned to work our program One Day at a Time. We were being taught that time can be our friend. Time is our Higher Power's way of not having everything happen at once.

Prayer for the Day

Higher Power, You are my teacher. You are in charge of the lesson. Help me accept this. Teach me how to use my time wisely.

Action for the Day

Today, I'll list five ways I use my time in ways that aren't helpful to me. I'll work at making time my friend.

*We are here to add what
we can to, not to get what
we can from, Life.*
— *Sir William Osler*

Service is a word we hear in our recovery program. *Service* means *work we do for others.* It's the backbone of our program. The reason is simple. Service to our Higher Power and to others breaks down our wanting to be self-centered.

Service brings us back into the world. We really are part of the group when we pitch in to make coffee, set up chairs, or talk in meetings. We really feel like part of the family when we run errands and help with meals and housework. We really connect with our Higher Power when we pray, "Use me today to help others." Service breaks down the feeling of being alone that being self-centered brings.

Prayer for the Day

Higher Power, help me to be of service to You and others. Show me what is needed.

Action for the Day

Today will be a service day. I'll look for where my skills are needed. I'll see how valued I am. I'll give to others, knowing that I, too, will receive.

*When I was about twelve, I
used to think I must be a
genius, but nobody's noticed.*
— *John Lennon*

We all have secret ideas about ourselves.
How often we have said to ourselves, *If only
they knew . . .* But if we watch others, we see
that many of their ideas are not so secret. We
can often guess how they see themselves by
the way they act. We all act out our secrets.

Faith means trusting our Higher Power
with our secrets. Faith in others means trusting them with our secret feelings.

Why share these secrets? When we were using alcohol or other drugs we lived too much
in a secret world. We need to give up the
secrets that keep us from others. We need
others in our lives. Our spirits *need* to be close
to others.

Prayer for the Day

God, help me to live in ways I'm not ashamed
to tell others. Allow me to meet you and others, free
of shame.

Action for the Day

Today I'll share one of my secrets with a loving
friend.

*There is no stronger bond
of friendship than a
mutual enemy.*
— *Frankfort Moore*

A.A. is a fellowship united against the same enemy—alcoholism. Our bonds give us strength to recover. We may not even know each other's last name, but we'll do anything to help each other stay sober.

Our illness has taken much. But it has also given us much. We have millions of new friends. Almost anywhere in the world, we can find a member of our fellowship. Our new way of life depends on the strength of the fellowship. We should do nothing to weaken it.

When you don't feel like going to a meeting—go, not only for yourself but for the sake of the fellowship. It truly needs you.

Prayer for the Day

Higher Power, You have given me A.A. Now help me to keep it going. A.A. needs me, just as I need A.A. Help me give even when I don't want to.

Action for the Day

Today, I'll give back to the program. I'll call a new member, volunteer to put on a meeting, or make the coffee.

Kindness in giving creates love.

> — Lao-tzu

In our illness, we were *takers*. Now, we've changed this around. We are now *givers*. Giving is a big part of recovery. Our word for it is *service*. Our program is based on care, respect, and service. Our program tells us to "practice these principles in all our affairs." No matter if it's getting to our meeting early to put on the coffee, or going on a Twelfth Step call, we are giving of ourselves. We give so that we know we can make a difference. We give so that we can know how to love better. The healing power of recovery is love. As we give love and kindness to others, we heal. Why? Because people grow by giving kindness and love to others.

Prayer for the Day

Higher Power, with Your help I'll be a kind and loving giver. I'll look for ways to share Your kindness.

Action for the Day

Today, I'll list five ways I can be of service to others. I'll put at least one of these ways into action today.

DECEMBER 11

When patterns are broken,
new worlds emerge.
— Tuli Kupferberg

Recovery has happened to us. We stopped drinking or using other drugs and, like magic, a new world appeared. Being sober sure shakes up a person's life!

It's good to shake up our world every now and then. This way, we see there's not just one "world," but many. We grow each time we step into a new world and learn new things. Of course, the addict's world was new and exciting to us at one time. But we got trapped and couldn't find our way out. Our Higher Power had to free us.

We need to try new worlds, but we always need to take our Higher Power with us—into worlds where there's honesty, love, and trust.

Prayer for the Day

Higher Power, lead me to new worlds where I'll learn more about living fully.

Action for the Day

I'll list three ways I can step into a new world today. For example, I could read something new, go to a museum, or eat a new food.

God gave us memory that
we might have roses in
December.
— James M. Barrie

Do you remember what it was like to not have sobriety? Remember the shame? Remember the loneliness? Remember lying and wishing you could stop? Remember the powerlessness?

Do you remember, also, how it felt when you began to believe you had an illness? Your shame was lifted. Remember what it was like to look around at your meeting and know you belonged? Your loneliness was lifted. Remember when your family started to trust you again? Your dishonesty had been lifted.

Sobriety gives us many roses. Our memory will help to keep them fresh.

Prayer for the Day

Higher Power, never let me forget what it was like. Why? Because I'm only one drink or pill away from losing You.

Action for the Day

I'll find a friend I trust I'll tell that person what my life was like before sobriety. I'll also talk about how I got sober.

Live and Let Live.
> — *AA slogan*

In our addiction, we didn't *care*. We didn't care about other people, even though we wanted to. We just didn't come through for them in ways that mattered. We didn't care for ourselves. We let bad things happen to us. And we didn't care about living. We set no goals, had no fun, smelled no flowers.

In our recovery, we do care. We care about others, ourselves, and life. Our spirits are on the move again. There's life in our hearts. Our bodies are getting well. And we're daring to dream.

We're living!

Prayer for the Day

Higher Power, put some life and energy into me today. Help me love my new life.

Action for the Day

Today, I'll focus on being alive. As I breathe in, I'll gather more and more life energy from nature.

*Hold fast to dreams for if
dreams die, life is a broken
winged bird that cannot
fly.*
— *Langston Hughes*

Many of our dreams died as our addiction got worse. We felt the loss but couldn't speak it. With recovery, we regain our ability to dream. Dreams of sharing our lives with family and friends return. They push out thoughts of getting high. Dreams of pride and self-respect reappear. They replace the awful feeling of shame.

Like the quote above says, "Hold fast to dreams. . . ." Our dreams are our wishes for the future. They hold a picture of who we want to be. In our dreams, we let our spirits soar. Often, we feel close to God, others, and ourselves. Thank God, we can dream again.

Prayer for the Day
Higher Power, thanks to you, my wings have been mended. Guide me as I fly.

Action for the Day
Today, I'll take time out to dream and share my dream with those I love.

*An ass is beautiful to an
ass, and a pig to a pig.*
— *English proverb*

When we see someone drunk and out of
control, can we see the beautiful person inside them? If we can't, who will? Step Twelve
reminds us that we have to help the alcoholic
or other drug addict who still suffers.

This task has been given to us because we,
most of all, should be able to look past the
drunkenness and see the person. We were
there. We know what it's like to be trapped in
a world without meaning. If these memories
have faded, we may need to go back over Step
One. We may find ourselves angry with the
practicing drunk or other drug addict. This
is a sign that we have gotten too far from our
past. Remember, "But for the grace of God ..."

Prayer for the Day

Higher Power, help me remember my past and
what it's like now. This helps me care about the
person who still suffers.

Action for the Day

Today, I'll respect my illness. I'll look for the
beauty inside every drunk and other drug addict.

*Charity sees the need, not
the cause.*
— *German proverb*

Charity is not just giving money to good causes. Charity is having a heart that's ready to give. Charity is helping a friend at two in the morning. Charity is going early to the meeting to put on coffee without being asked. *Service* is how Twelve Step programs refer to "charity." Service and charity are a lifestyle. We see a need, so we try to help. Our values and our heart will guide us in how we help.

Service is a big part of our program. Service helps us think of others, not just of ourselves. We stop asking, "What's in it for me?" The act of helping others is what's in it for us. Sobriety is what's in it for us. Serenity is what's in it for us.

Prayer for the Day
Higher Power, You have given me many talents. Help me see how my talents can make the world a better place. Giving of myself is believing in You and myself.

Action for the Day
Today, I'll list my talents and I'll think of ways I can use them to help others.

The rose and the thorn,
and sorrow and gladness
are linked together.

— *Saadi*

When we were drinking and drugging, we didn't have to deal much with feelings. We turned them off. Then, when we let go of the alcohol and other drugs, we started to come back to life. Now—we have feelings again!

But even now, in recovery, we're scared of too much happiness. It's true—we don't want sadness and pain at all. Yet, feelings—the good and the bad—keep on coming.

And we have to handle them. We *are* learning to handle our feelings. We're getting strong enough to deal with them. With the help of our friends in the program, and our Higher Power, we're ready for life.

Prayer for the Day

Higher Power, I want to be fully alive, but I'm a little scared. Help me know what to do with my feelings today.

Action for the Day

Today, I'll be open to feelings. I'll enjoy my good feelings and share them. I'll ask for help with hard feelings by praying, and by calling my sponsor.

The only thing we have to
fear is fear itself.
— Franklin D. Roosevelt

As addicts, we had lots of fear. Some of us were afraid of failure. So we didn't try to do much. Or else we tried too hard all the time. We used alcohol and other drugs to forget our fear, but it didn't go away. It got worse.

Now we know we don't have to be afraid. When our lives are in the care of our Higher Power, we're safe. Faith is the cure for our fear.

But still, fear keeps creeping back inside us. That's okay. It's normal. There is so much that's new in our sober life! We don't know what will happen next. It's hard to always remember to trust our Higher Power. It's hard to always do what our Higher Power says. It's hard to always have faith. We have to practice turning our fear over to our Higher Power.

Prayer for the Day

Higher Power, be with me when I'm afraid. Help me remember to have faith to believe in You, even when my fear tells me not to.

Action for the Day

Today, I'll notice my fear and pray each time I get afraid.

*The truth is more
important than the facts.*
— *Frank Lloyd Wright*

Before recovery, we relied on false facts about addiction. We said things like: "I can quit anytime I want." "If you had my family, you'd drink too." The truth is, we were out of control. We couldn't manage our lives. We were sick. We were scared. When others pointed out this truth to us, we denied it.

Honesty, the backbone of our program, is about *truth.* We even start our meetings with the truth about who we are. "Hi, my name is _____, and I'm an alcoholic," or "Hi, my name is _____, and I'm a drug addict." The truth frees us from our addiction. The truth heals us and gives us comfort. It's like a blanket on a cold winter night.

Prayer for the Day

Higher Power, help me be an honest person. I pray for the strength to face the truth and speak it.

Action for the Day

Today, I'll list three ways I have used facts in a dishonest way.

*There are two ways of
spreading light: to be the
candle or the mirror that
reflects it.*
— *Edith Wharton*

Our Higher Power is the candle. And our
hearts, like a mirror, reflect a warm, loving
glow.

But when we used alcohol and other drugs,
we tried to be the candle. We wanted to have
control. Many of us acted like this to hide how
out of control we felt. We never thought we
could be happy by admitting we were out of
control.

In recovery, we accept that it's okay to be
the mirror. We accept that our Higher Power
is the candle that guides us. We want to be
the mirror that reflects how much our Higher
Power loves us.

Prayer for the Day

Higher Power, thank-you for the light and
warmth You give me.

Action for the Day

Tonight, I'll light a candle and place it in front
of a mirror. I'll study how they work together to
light the room.

Don't give your advice
before you are called upon.
— Desiderius Erasmus

If someone wants your advice, the person will ask for it. That's one reason why in Twelve Step programs we don't go around trying to talk people into joining.

But people will ask us for advice. They'll see how we've changed, and they'll want what we have. All we have to do is tell them where we found it—in AA, NA, or another Twelve Step group. We don't tell them what to do. We tell them our own story—what it was like, what happened, and where we are now.

And we invite them to join us.

Prayer for the Day

Higher Power, help me carry the healing message of the program to those who ask for my advice.

Action for the Day

I'll make a decision to spend time with the next person who asks for my help.

*It is possible to be different
and still be all right.*
— *Anne Wilson Schaef*

Each of us is special. In some ways, we're all different. It's a good thing too. We'd be bored if we were all the same.

Sometimes, though, we try to hide the special things about us. We don't want to be "different." But the ways that we're different make us special. Some of us have a good sense of humor. Others have a knack of fixing things. Some of us make beautiful art. Others are great with kids. Our Higher Power made us as different, as unique, as beautiful snowflakes.

Prayer for the Day

Higher Power, help me use my special gifts the way You want me to. Help me be thankful that You have given me something special to share with others.

Action for the Day

I'll think of one thing about me that's special. I'll talk with my sponsor about it.

*We not only need to be
willing to give, but also to
be open to receiving from
others.*

— *from* On Hope

Many of us took so much from others during our addiction that now we may not want to ask for anything. We may be afraid to ask for help, so our needs go unmet. In fact, many of us would now rather give than receive.

In recovery, we need to understand the difference between *taking* and *receiving*. Giving to others is important. So is receiving from others. As we grow spiritually, we learn to accept gifts. The gift of sobriety teaches us this. We need to accept the gifts the world gives us without shame. We are entitled. God loves us and will give us much if we're willing to receive it.

Prayer for the Day

Higher Power, help me be receptive to Your gifts. Help me see and believe that I'm entitled to all the happiness of the world.

Action for the Day

I'll think of what a friend has given me. I'll thank this friend

*We must all hang together
or we will hang separately.*
— Benjamin Franklin

We didn't get ourselves sober. And we don't keep ourselves sober. Our program does this. This is why the Twelfth Step is so important. We must be willing to give service to our program *whenever* it's needed. When a friend calls and says he or she feels like using, we don't just say we're sorry. We go get our friend and take him or her to a meeting. Our survival depends on this kind of action.

We are to carry the message. We carry the message by deeds, not words. We are part of a fellowship based on action. A fellowship guided by love. It is not words that keep us sober—it is action.

Prayer for the Day

Higher Power, help me be ready whenever there's a need. Help me be ready to put my self-will aside. Give me strength.

Action for the Day

I will think of my group members. Who could use a supportive call or visit? I will call or visit those who need my help.

*To love is to place our
happiness in the happiness
of another.*
— *Gottfried Wilhelm
von Leibnitz*

Now that we're getting well, we feel the need for love more than ever. We tried to avoid love by using chemicals to feel good. But it didn't work. Addiction cut us off even more from people.

How do we fill our need for love? We can think about this fact: People give us love all the time. Only we just haven't seen it. Every time someone comes to a meeting to get well with us, that is love. Love isn't all-or-nothing. Little gems of love are all over. Watch for them. Enjoy them. Give them to others.

Prayer for the Day

Higher Power, love comes from You. Help me see it, feel it, and give it.

Action for the Day

I'll look three persons in the eye today and send them love in my smile.

To be emotionally committed to somebody is very difficult, but to be alone is impossible.
— *Stephen Sondheim*

Let's face it, relationships are hard work! But we are lucky! Recovery is *about* relationships. We learn how to set limits. We learn how to listen to and talk to others. In Step One, we begin a new relationship with ourselves. In Steps Two and Three, we begin a relationship with our Higher Power. In later Steps, we mend our relationships with family and friends.

In our relationship with our sponsor, we learn about being friends. And our past relationship with alcohol and other drugs is being replaced by people and our Higher Power.

Prayer for the Day
Higher Power, thank-you for all my new relationships. Thank-you for teaching me how to feel human again.

Action for the Day
Today, I'll make a list of all the new relationships I have now, due to my sobriety.

*Reading is to the Mind,
what exercise is to the
Body.*
— *Joseph Addison*

Good ideas are the seeds that start our growth. We hear things at meetings. We listen to our sponsor. Maybe we listen to program tapes. And we read.

Reading is special, because we do it when we're alone. We read in quiet times, when we can think. We can read as fast or as slowly as we want. We can mark special words and come back to them again and again. We'll figure things out in our own way, but we need help to get started. That's why we read. It gives us good ideas to think about.

Prayer for the Day

Higher Power, speak to me through helpful readings and help me learn at my best pace.

Action for the Day

Reading is easier the more I do it. Today I'll feel proud that I've read program ideas to get my mind thinking in a healthy way.

*If you will walk with lame
men you'll soon limp
yourself.*
— *Seamas MacManus*

Before recovery, we kept company with people who were as sick as us, or worse. We got angry and made fun of people who were trying to improve their lives. They scared us. They were like mirrors that reflected how spiritually lost we were becoming.

Now we walk in the crowd we avoided. Now we have values. We have spiritual beliefs. Living up to these values and beliefs can be hard. We need to be around people who live by their values.

In recovery, we learn that we need others. Remember, the first word in Step One is *we*. We need good people in our lives. We need friends who will not just tell us what we want to hear, but what we are doing wrong.

Prayer for the Day
Sometimes I act like I need no one. Help me pick my friends wisely, for my life is at stake.

Action for the Day
Today, I'll pick one friend, and we'll talk about how we can better help each other.

> *Many people are living in*
> *an emotional jail without*
> *recognizing it.*
> — *Virginia Satir*

Our disease was our jail. We felt so bad that we were sure we must have done something awful. But we didn't cause our disease. We have done nothing to deserve our disease. We aren't responsible for the fact that we have a disease.

But we *are* responsible for our recovery. We have been granted probation. The terms of our probation are simple: don't drink or use other drugs, and work the Steps. If we follow these simple rules, we'll be free. And it will be clear to us that only a Power greater than ourselves could give us this freedom.

Prayer for the Day

Higher Power, help me to stay free. For this next twenty-four-hour period, take from me any urge to drink or use other drugs. With Your help, I'll be free.

Action for the Day

Today, I'll think about my disease. I am not morally weak. I have a dangerous illness. What can keep me free from my disease?

Keep It Simple.
— *AA slogan*

Addiction messed up our thinking. We know that from taking Step One. We forgot things. We had blackouts. We made excuses, and we even started to believe them. We were mixed up. We couldn't figure things out. We decided to get high and forget about it.

Now, our minds are clear. We can keep thinking clearly if we work our program and Keep It Simple. Don't drink or use other drugs. Go to meetings. Work the Steps. Be yourself. Ask for help. Trust your Higher Power.

Two thoughts will always mess us up if we let them in. They are "Yes, but..." and "What if?" Don't let them in. Keep It Simple.

Prayer for the Day

Higher Power, thanks for recovery. Help me stay sober and clean today.

Action for the Day

Today, I'll take one thing at a time and Keep It Simple.

*May you live all the days of
your life.*
— *Jonathan Swift*

Tonight, at midnight, a new year will begin.
None of us know what the new year will hold.
But we can trust ourselves to hold on to the
spirit of recovery as we go through the year.
As a new year is about to begin, we can re-
joice in our new way of life. We can give our
will and our life to our Higher Power. By doing
these things, we'll be ready for the new year.

Prayer for the Day
Higher Power, I pray that I'll start the new year
safe in Your loving arms. I pray that I'll keep working my program.

Action for the Day
Tonight, at midnight, I'll say the Serenity Prayer.
I will think of all the others who have read this
meditation book and who will join me in my prayer.
We are a recovering community.

THE TWELVE STEPS
OF ALCOHOLICS ANONYMOUS*

1. We admitted we were powerless over alcohol—that our lives had become unmanageable.
2. Came to believe that a Power greater than ourselves could restore us to sanity.
3. Made a decision to turn our will and our lives over to the care of God *as we understood Him.*
4. Made a searching and fearless moral inventory of ourselves.
5. Admitted to God, to ourselves, and to another human being the exact nature of our wrongs.
6. Were entirely ready to have God remove all these defects of character.
7. Humbly asked Him to remove our shortcomings.
8. Made a list of all persons we had harmed, and became willing to make amends to them all.
9. Made direct amends to such people wherever possible, except when to do so would injure them or others.
10. Continued to take personal inventory and when we were wrong promptly admitted it.
11. Sought through prayer and meditation to improve our conscious contact with God *as we understood Him,* praying only for knowledge of His will for us and the power to carry that out.
12. Having had a spiritual awakening as the result of these steps, we tried to carry this message to alcoholics, and to practice these principles in all our affairs.

---

*The Twelve Steps of AA are taken from *Alcoholics Anonymous* (Third Edition), and published by AA World Services, Inc., New York, N.Y., 59-60. Reprinted with permission.

THE TWELVE TRADITIONS
OF ALCOHOLICS ANONYMOUS*

1. Our common welfare should come first; personal recovery depends upon A.A. unity.
2. For our group purpose there is but one ultimate authority—a loving God as He may express Himself in our group conscience. Our leaders are but trusted servants—they do not govern.
3. The only requirement for A.A. membership is a desire to stop drinking.
4. Each group should be autonomous, except in matters affecting other groups or A.A. as a whole.
5. Each group has but one primary purpose—to carry its message to the alcoholic who still suffers.
6. An A.A. group ought never endorse, finance, or lend the A.A. name to any related facility or outside enterprise lest problems of money, property and prestige divert us from our primary purpose.
7. Every A.A. group ought to be fully self-supporting, declining outside contributions.
8. Alcoholics Anonymous should remain forever nonprofessional, but our service centers may employ special workers.
9. A.A., as such, ought never to be organized, but we may create service boards or committees directly responsible to those they serve.
10. Alcoholics Anonymous has no opinion on outside issues, hence the A.A. name ought never be drawn into public controversy.
11. Our public relations policy is based on attraction rather than promotion; we need always maintain personal anonymity at the level of press, radio, television and films.
12. Anonymity is the spiritual foundation of all our traditions, ever reminding us to place principles before personalities.

*The Twelve Traditions of AA are taken from *Twelve Steps and Twelve Traditions,* published by AA World Services, Inc., New York, N.Y., 129-87. Reprinted with permission.

THE SERENITY PRAYER

God grant me the serenity
To accept the things I cannot change,
The courage to change the things I can,
And the wisdom to know the difference.

INDEX

NOTES

NOTES

NOTES

NOTES

NOTES

NOTES

NOTES

NOTES

NOTES

NOTES

NOTES

NOTES

Other titles that will interest you...

Twenty-Four Hours a Day

Few books touch—and help to change—as many lives as this one. Now the world's best-known collection of A.A. wisdom is available in a comfortable-to-hold, easy-to-take along paperback edition. Each day, it provides a brief thought, meditation, and prayer for living well and staying sober the next twenty-four hours. For those new to recovery, or looking for program renewal, *Twenty-Four Hours a Day* is a guide to the power of prayer and a strong spiritual relationship with the God of your understanding. 400 pp.
Order No. 5093

Day by Day
Daily Meditations for Recovering Addicts

"God help me to stay clean and sober today!" is the core of each daily meditation. This message supports and reinforces the fundamental principles of N.A., C.A., and other Twelve Step programs. Daily goal exercises bring recovery skills actively to the forefront. 400 pp.
Order No. 1081

For price and order information, or a free catalog, please call our Telephone Representatives.

HAZELDEN

1-800-328-0098
(24-Hour Toll Free.
U.S., Canada, and the
Virgin Islands)

1-612-257-4010
(Outside the U.S.
and Canada)

1-612-257-1331
(24-Hour FAX)

Pleasant Valley Road • P.O. Box 176 • Center City, MN 55012-0176